FUNKO STYLE

Boy and Girl Fashion Models

belongs to:

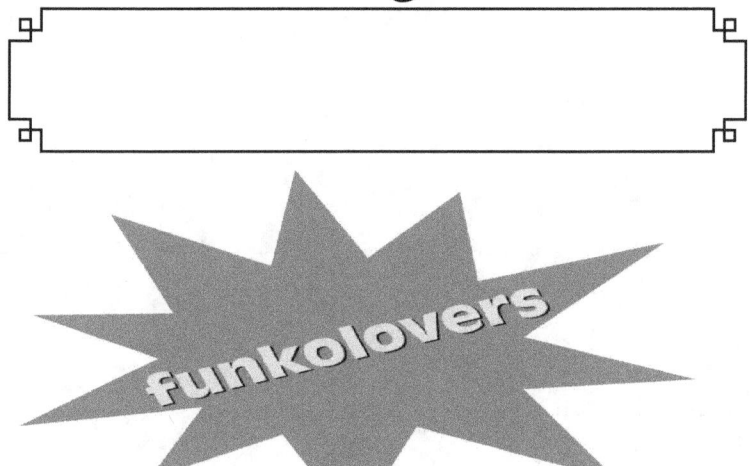

REGULAR PRACTICE IS KEY TO IMPROVING YOUR SKILLS

RECOMMENDATIONS

1. Try to keep your wrist steady and stable as you draw to produce crisp, precise strokes.
Practice rotating your wrist to create smoother curves.
2. Draw crosshatching lines over an area can create interesting texture and add dimension to a drawing.
3. Apply different levels of pressure to the tracing to produce different tones and textures.
4. Add shadows and highlights to create depth and dimension. Adding shadows and highlights to a drawing can make it appear more realistic and three-dimensional.
Learn to use light and shadow to create effects of depth and to make objects appear bulkier.
5. If you need to make corrections, do so. Use an eraser to remove unwanted strokes; or correction pencil, as needed.

INSTRUCTIONS

It's fun to bring your creations to life, add color to them. Color the skin, clothes and accessories as you want. Draw the environment, the background that you want.

MATERIALS

Pencils, pens, markers, nibs, highlighters, eraser, correction pencil, rules, and others that you prefer.

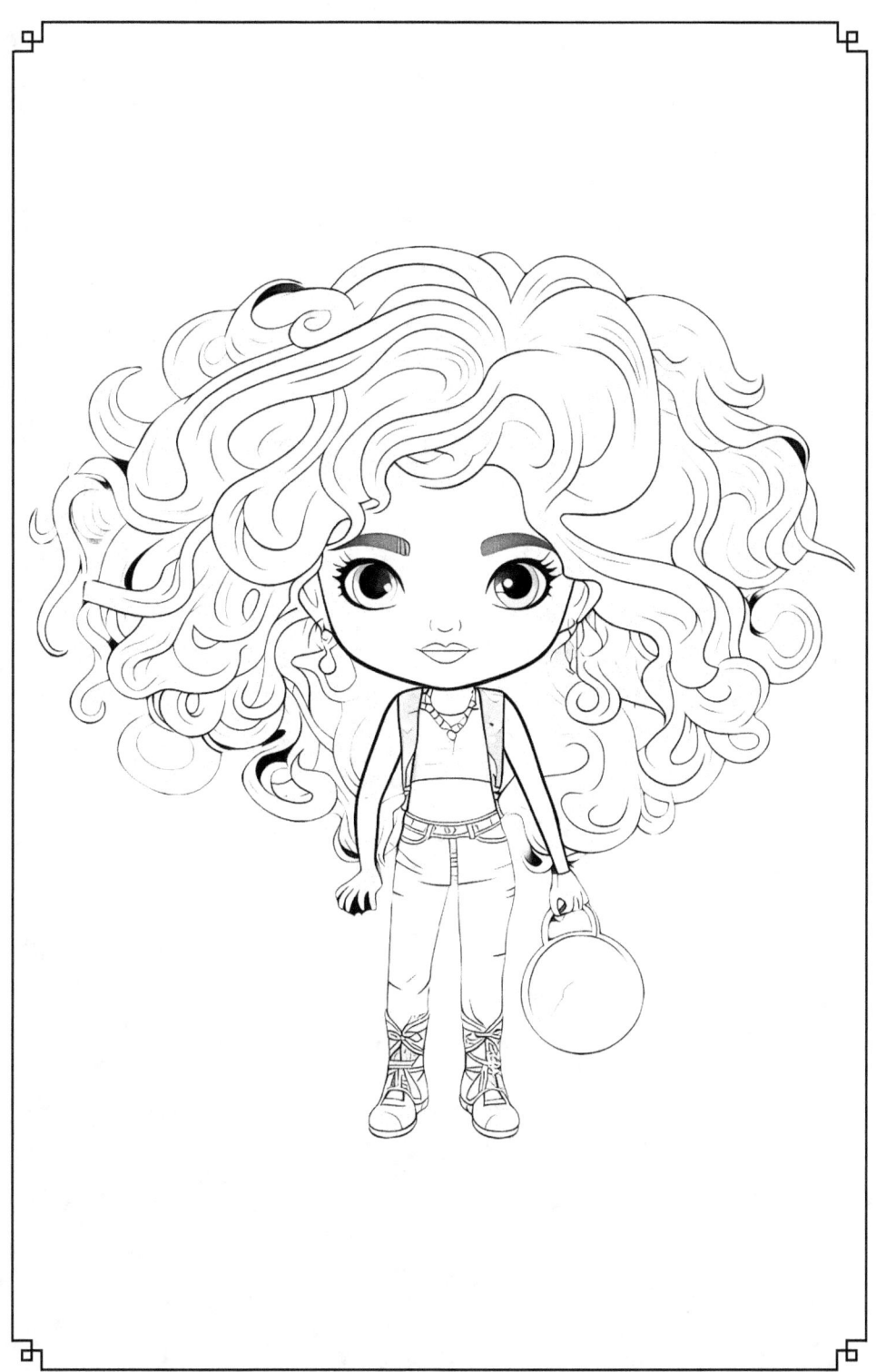

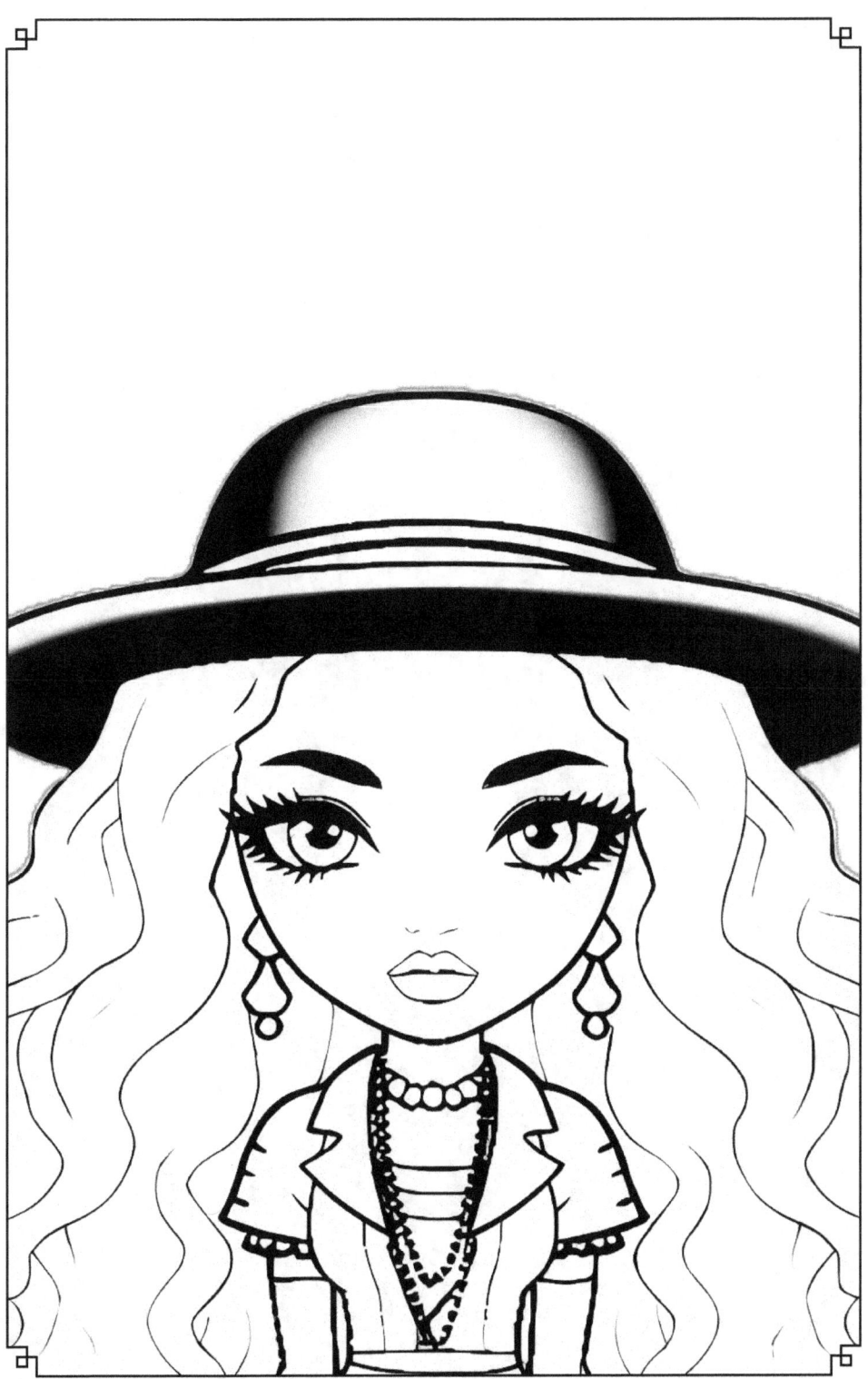

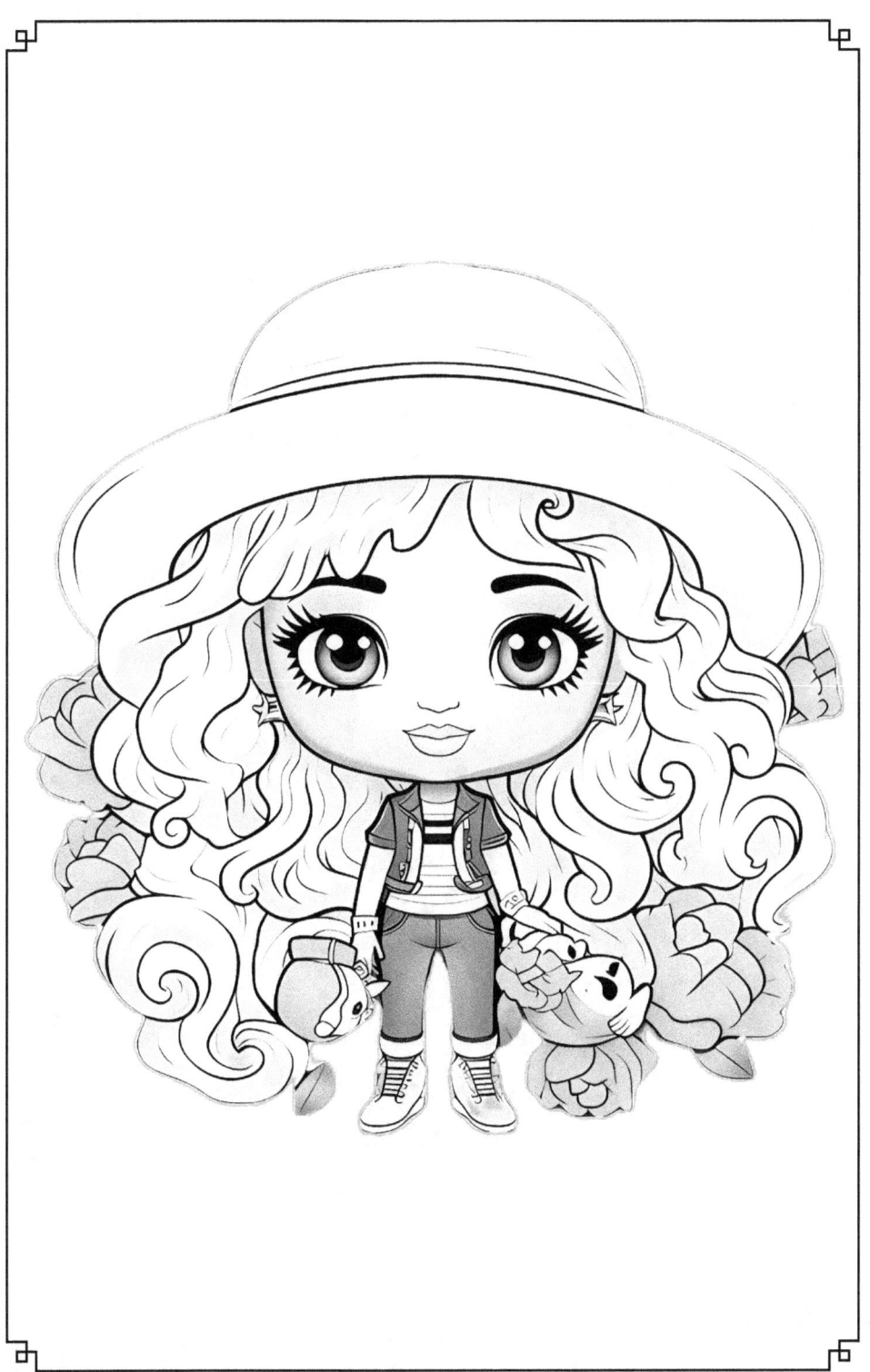

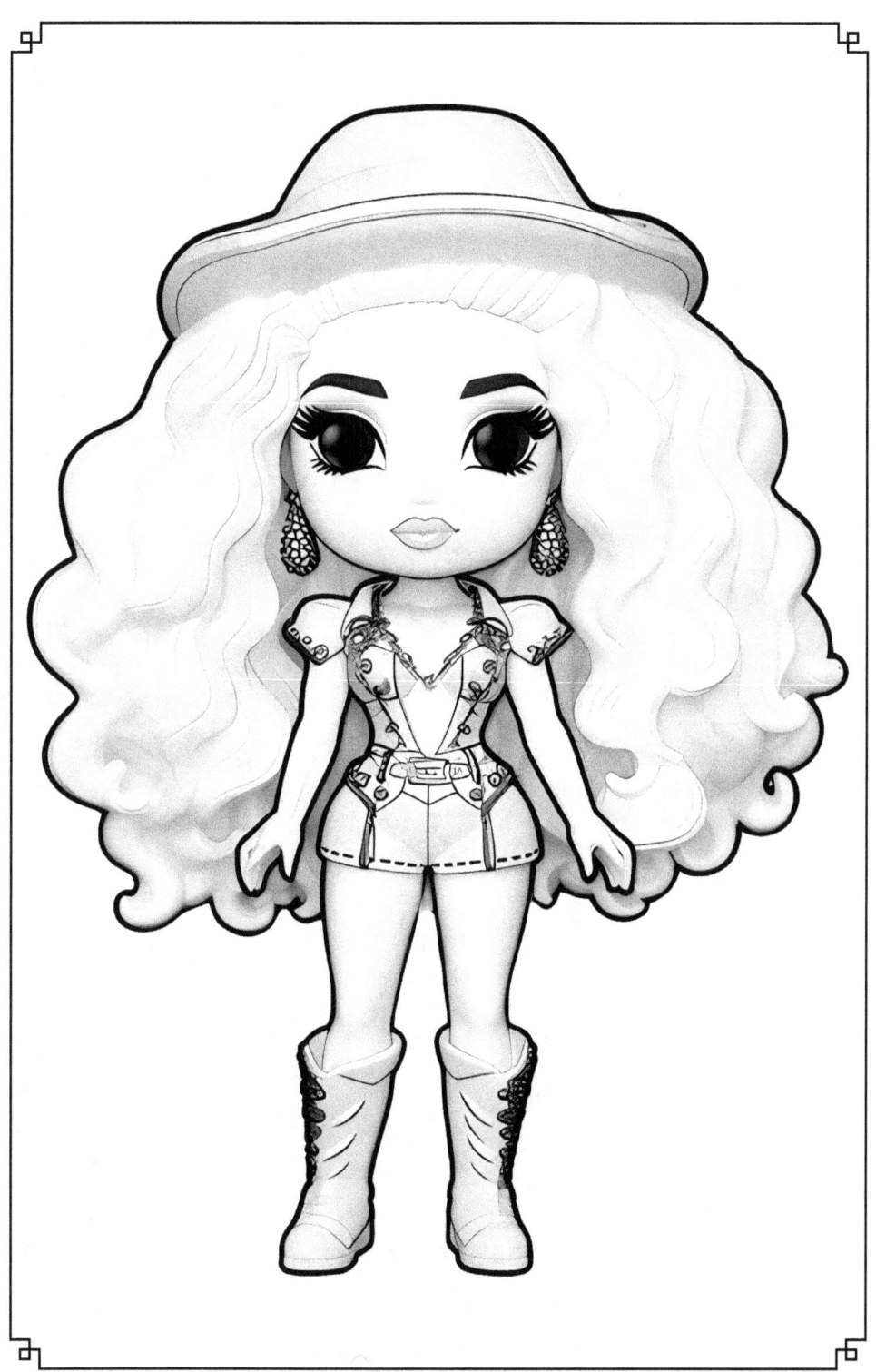

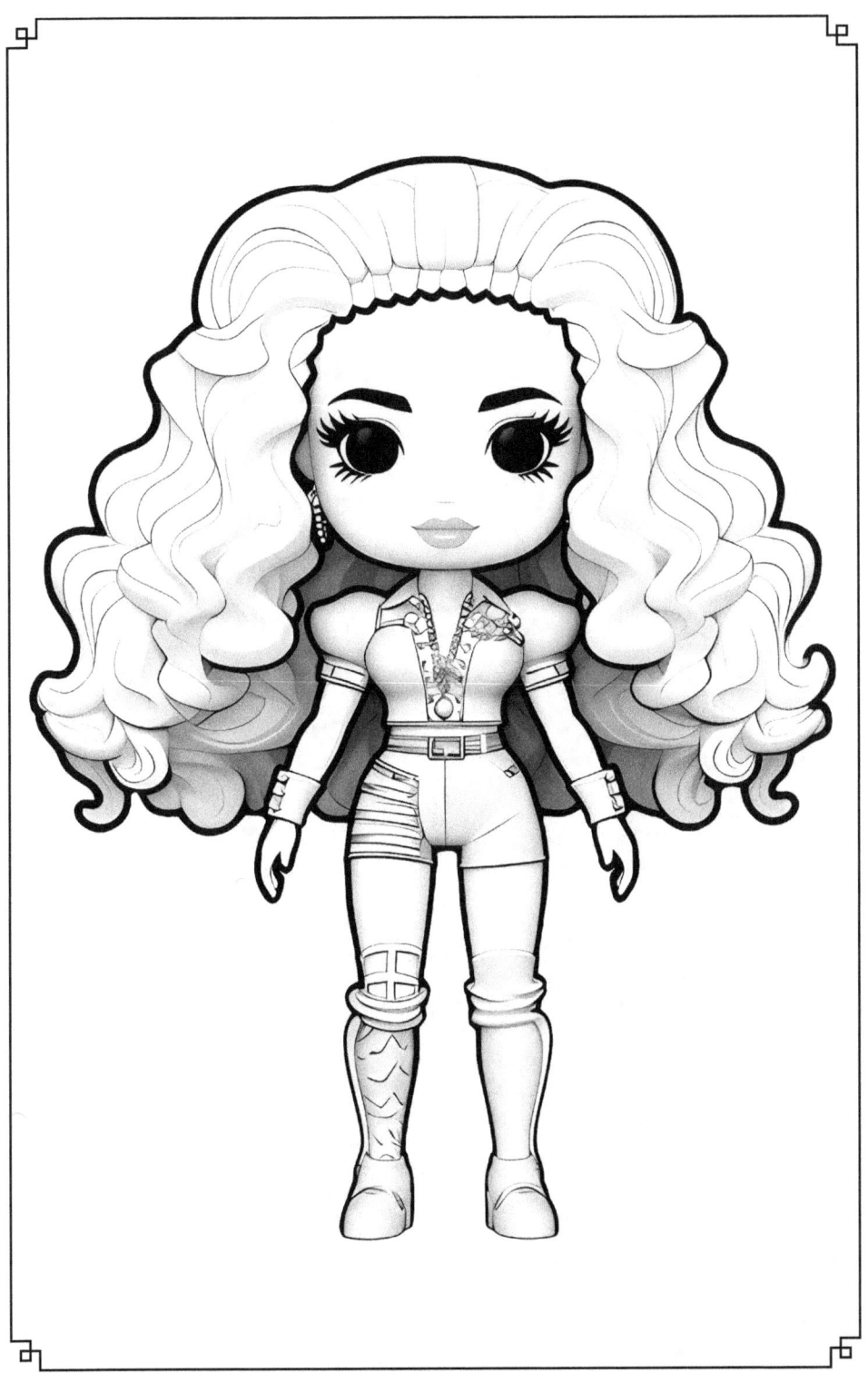

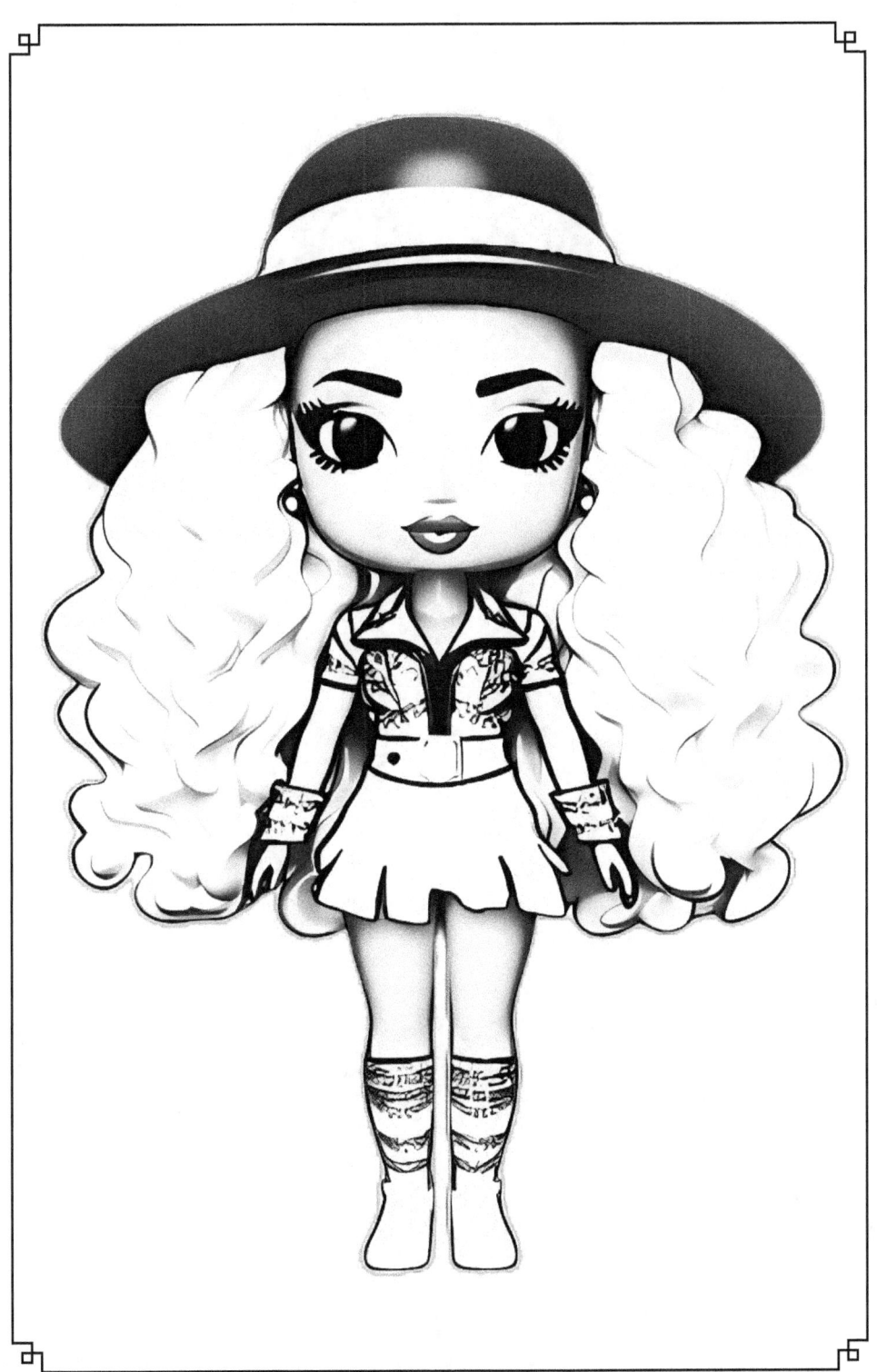

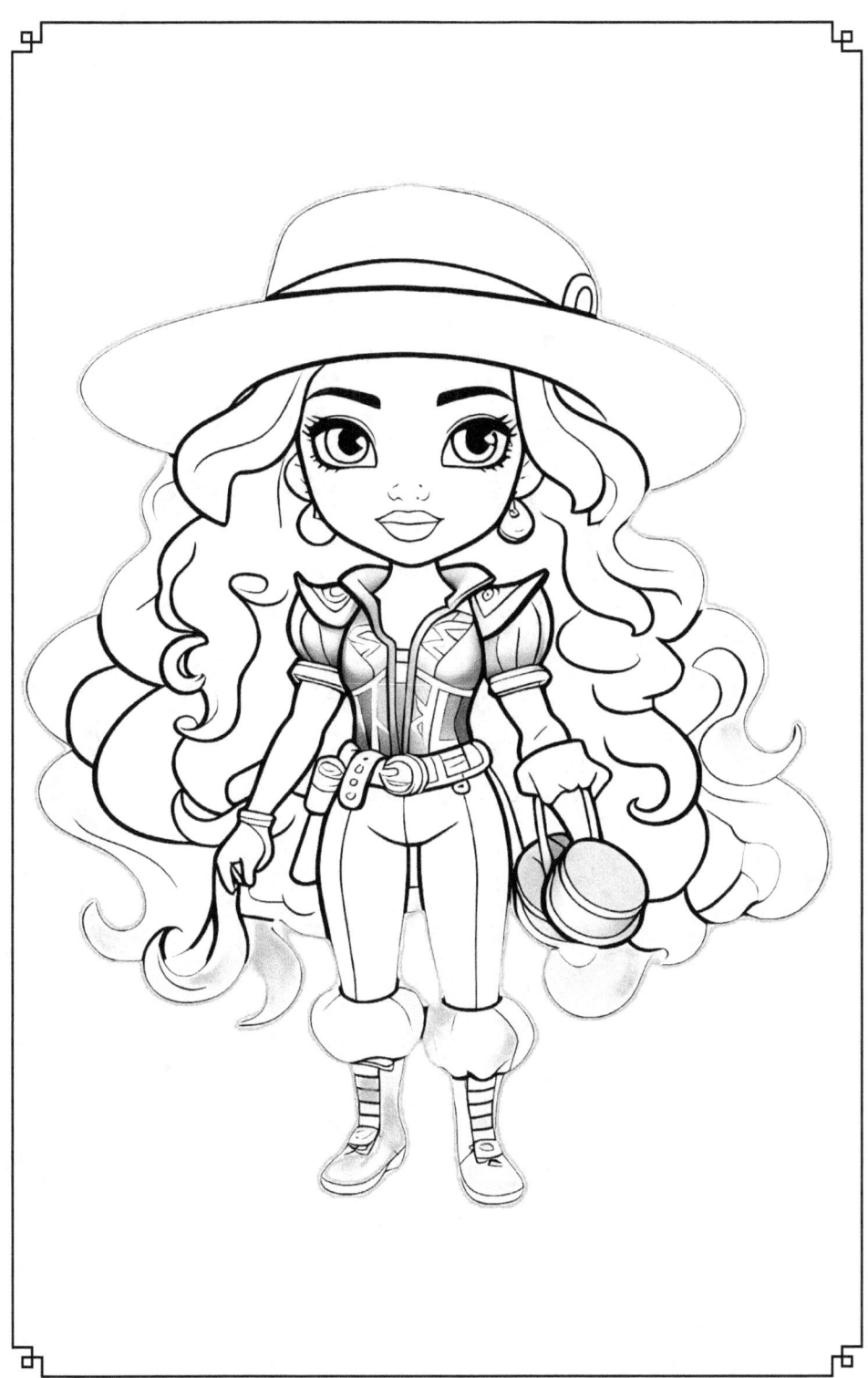

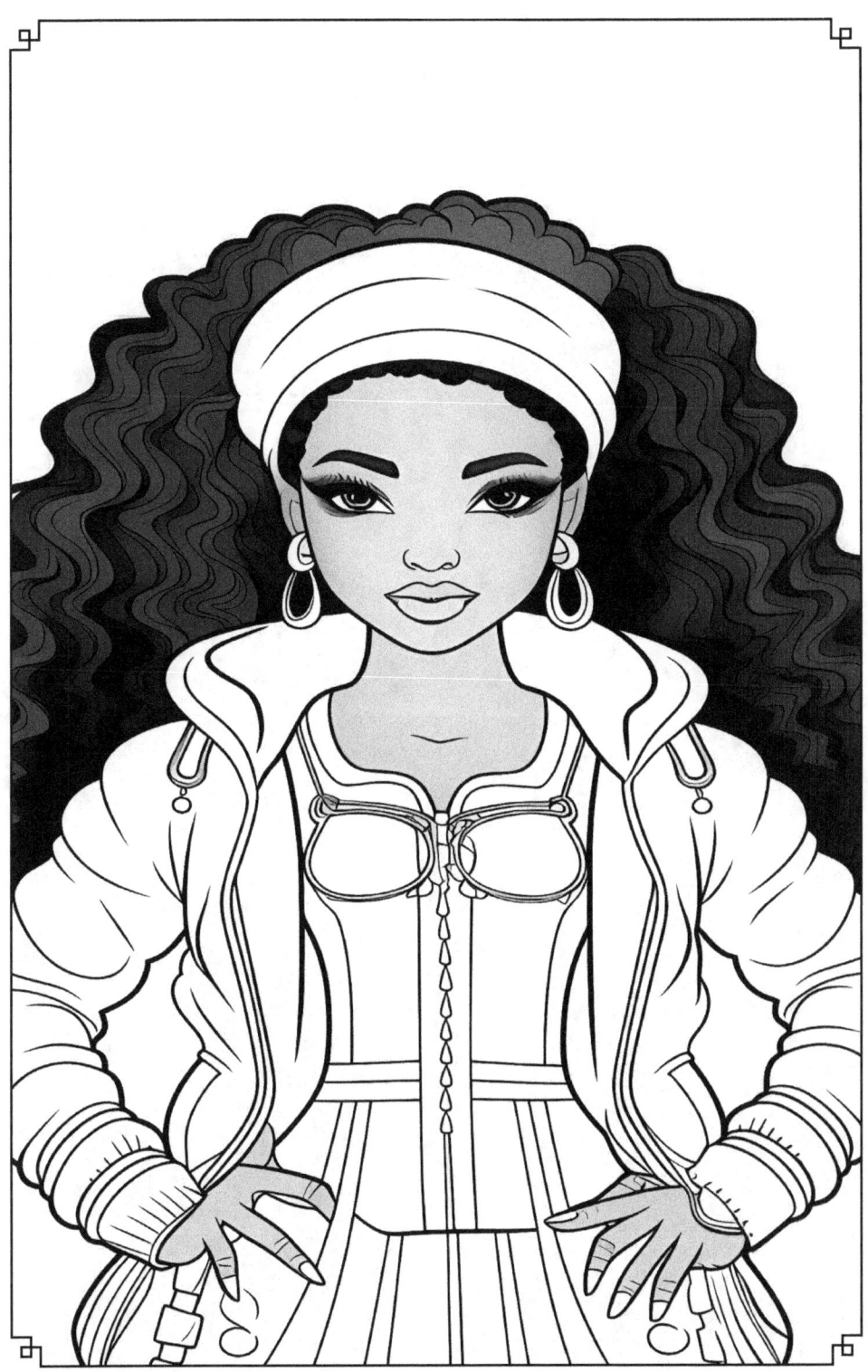

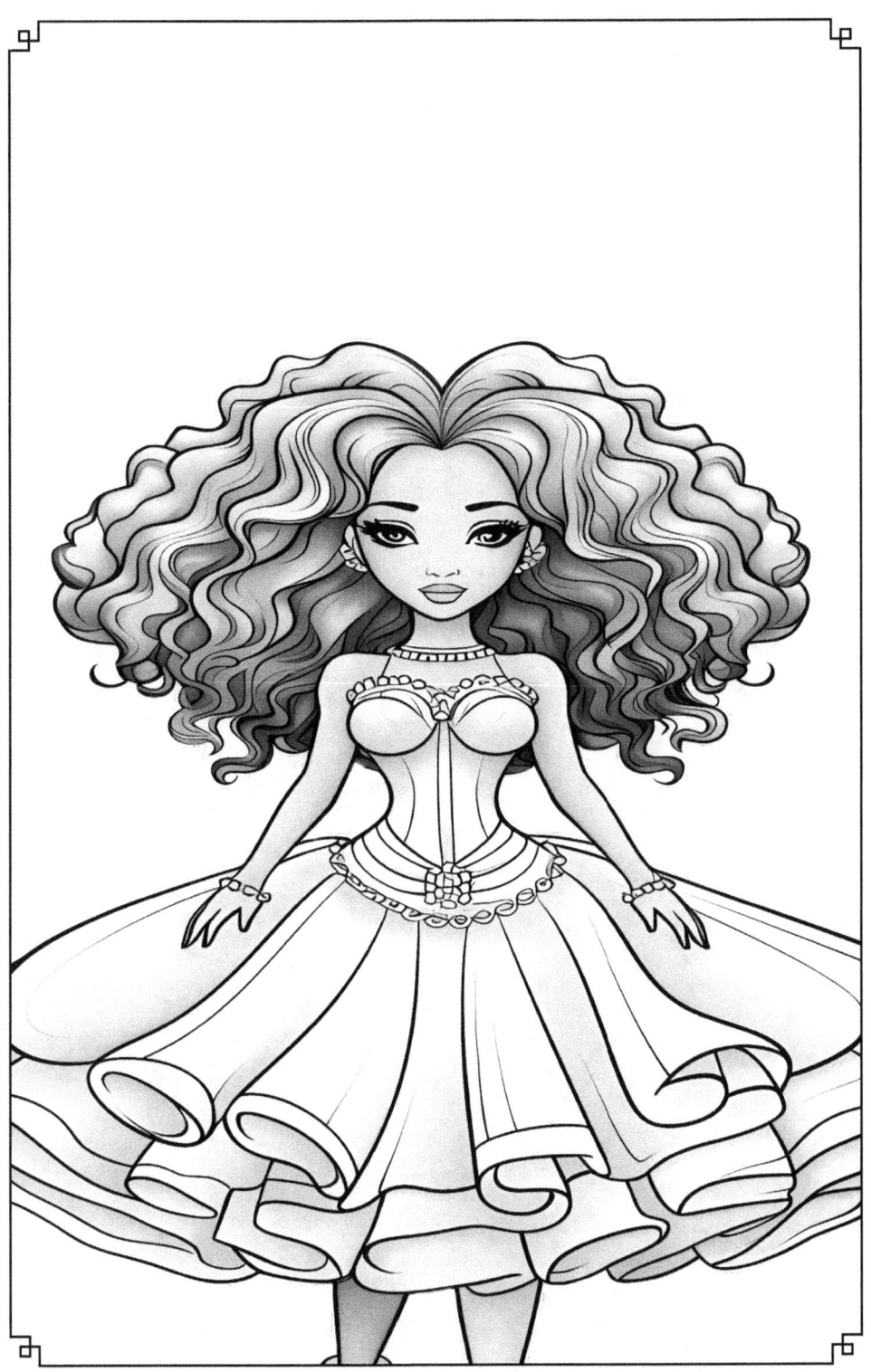

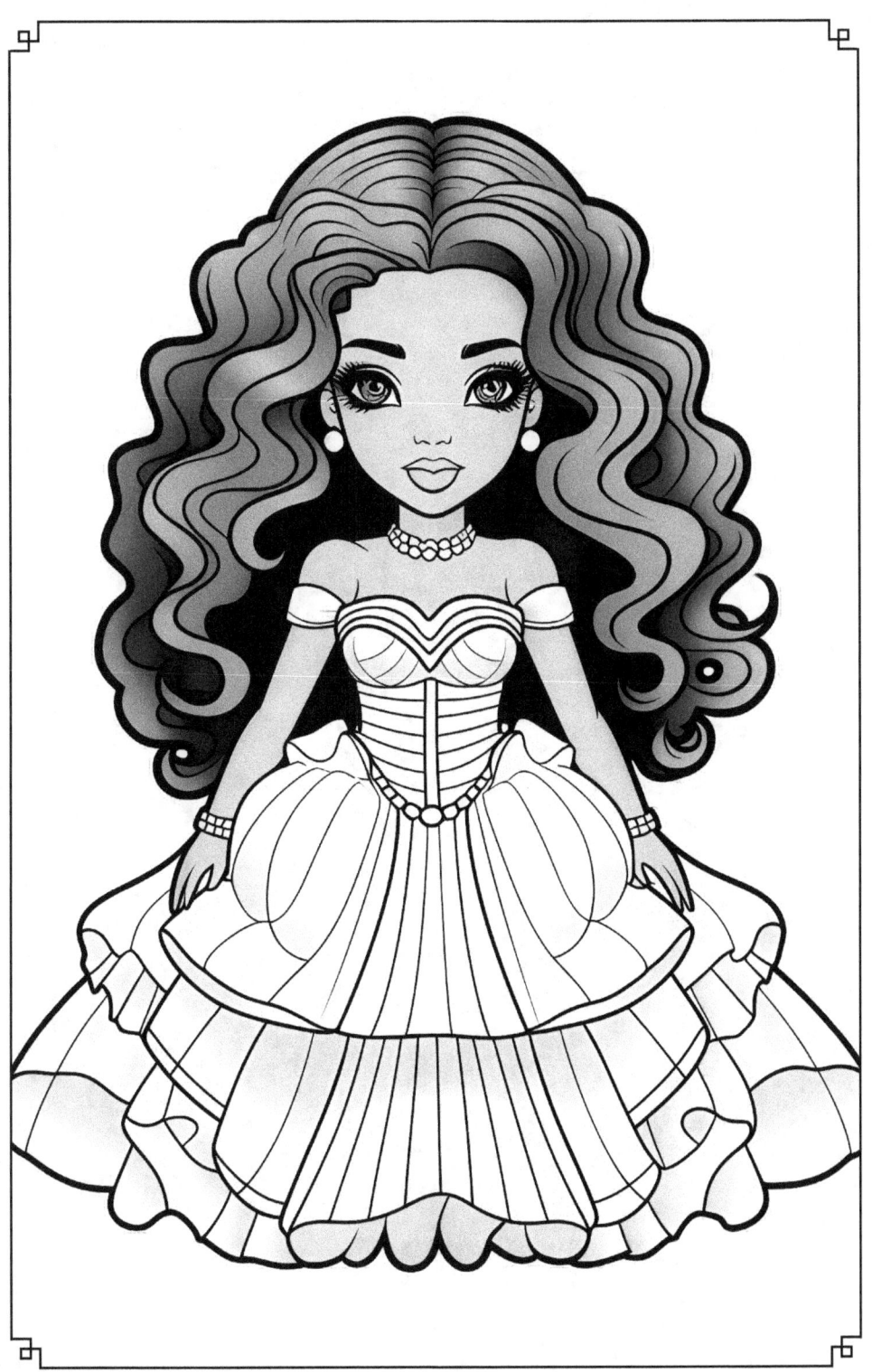

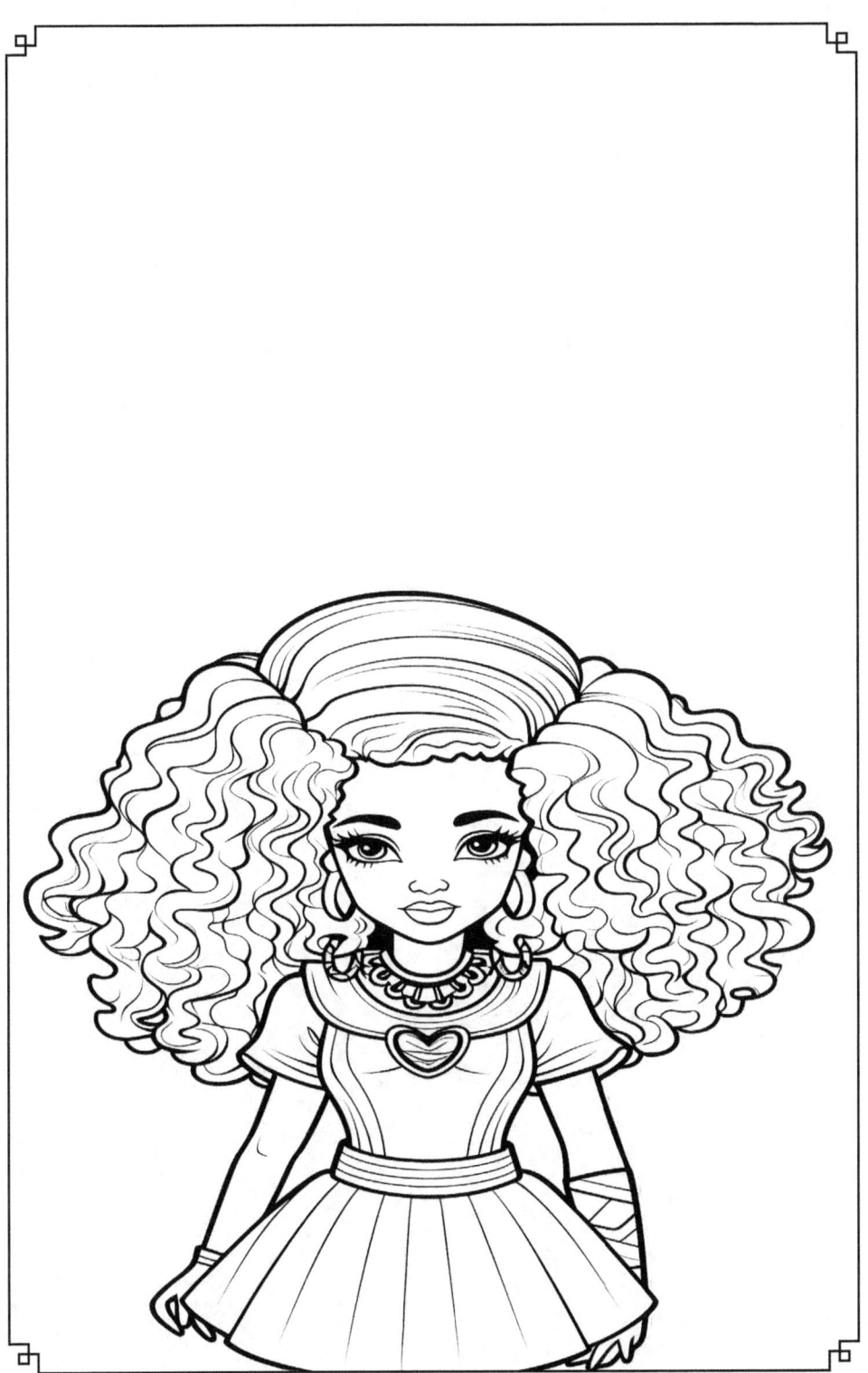

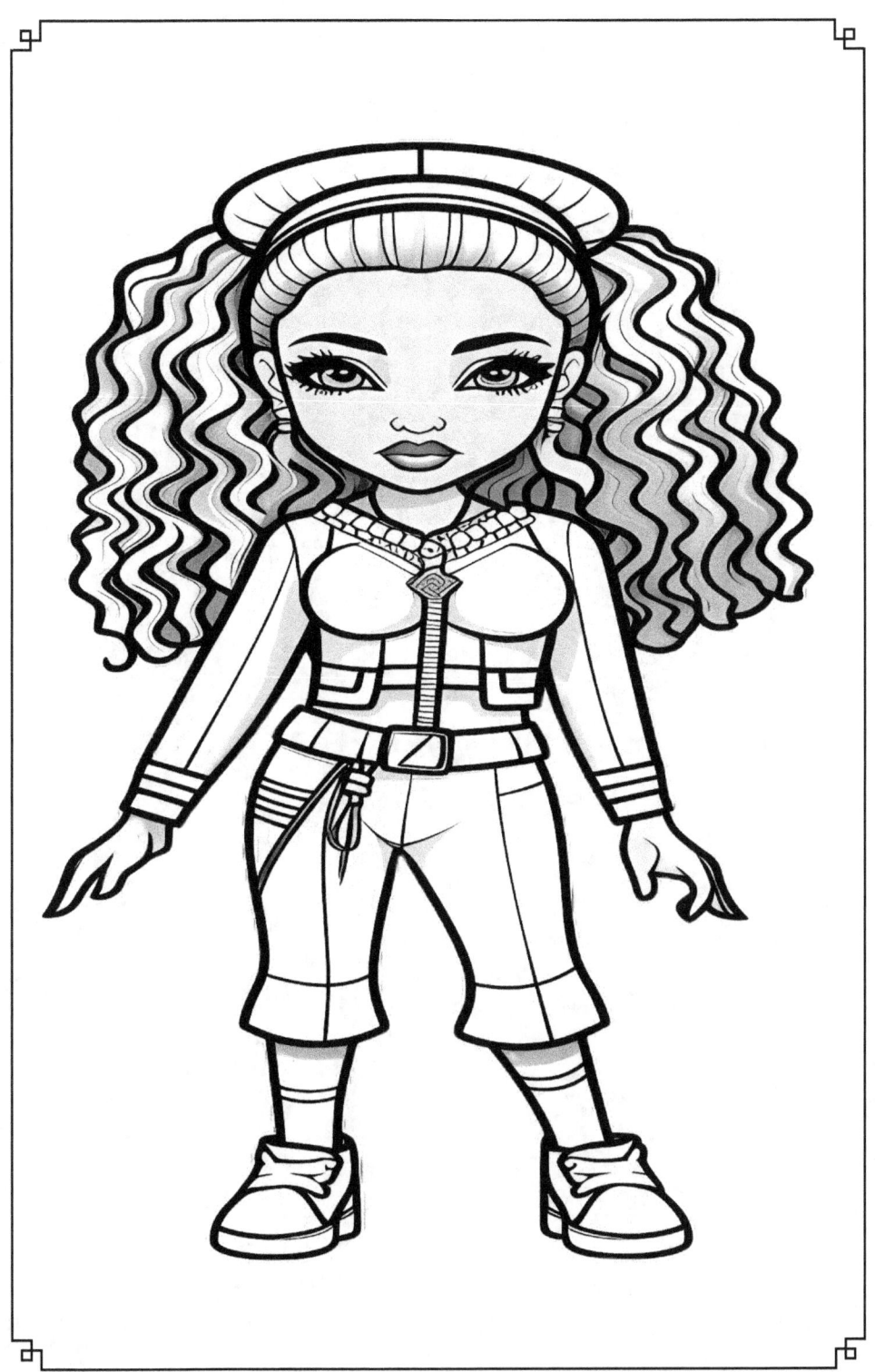

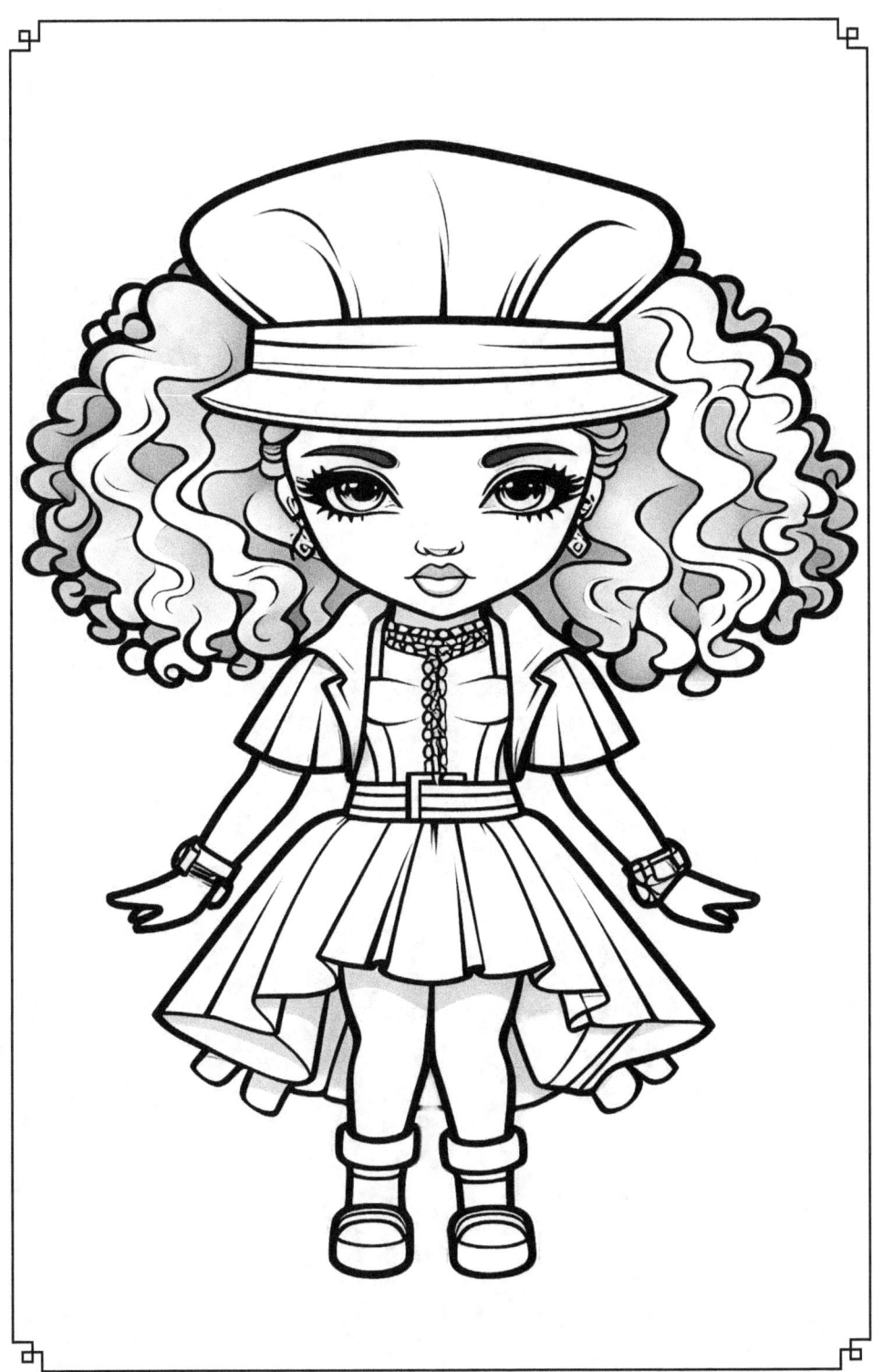

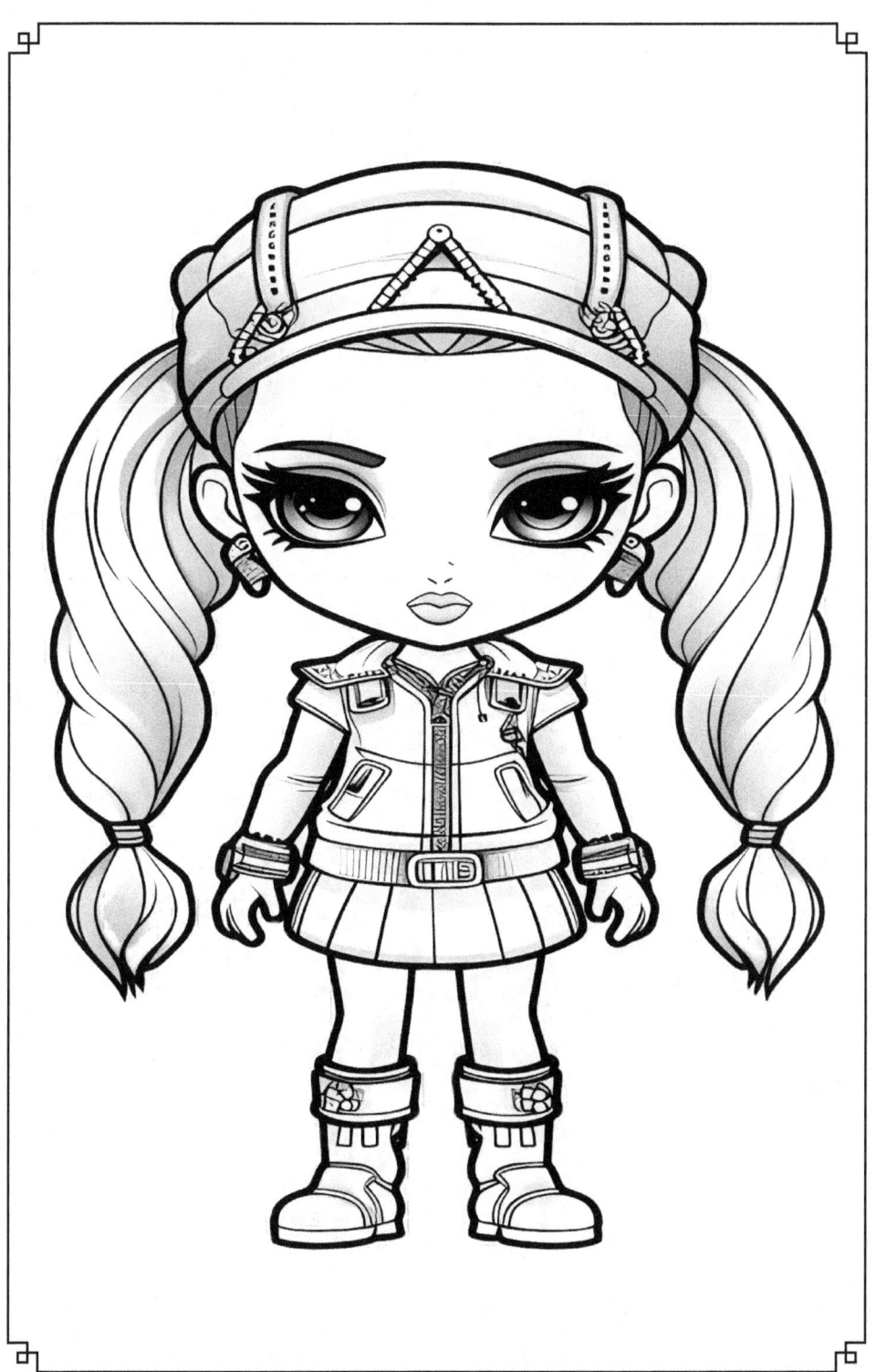

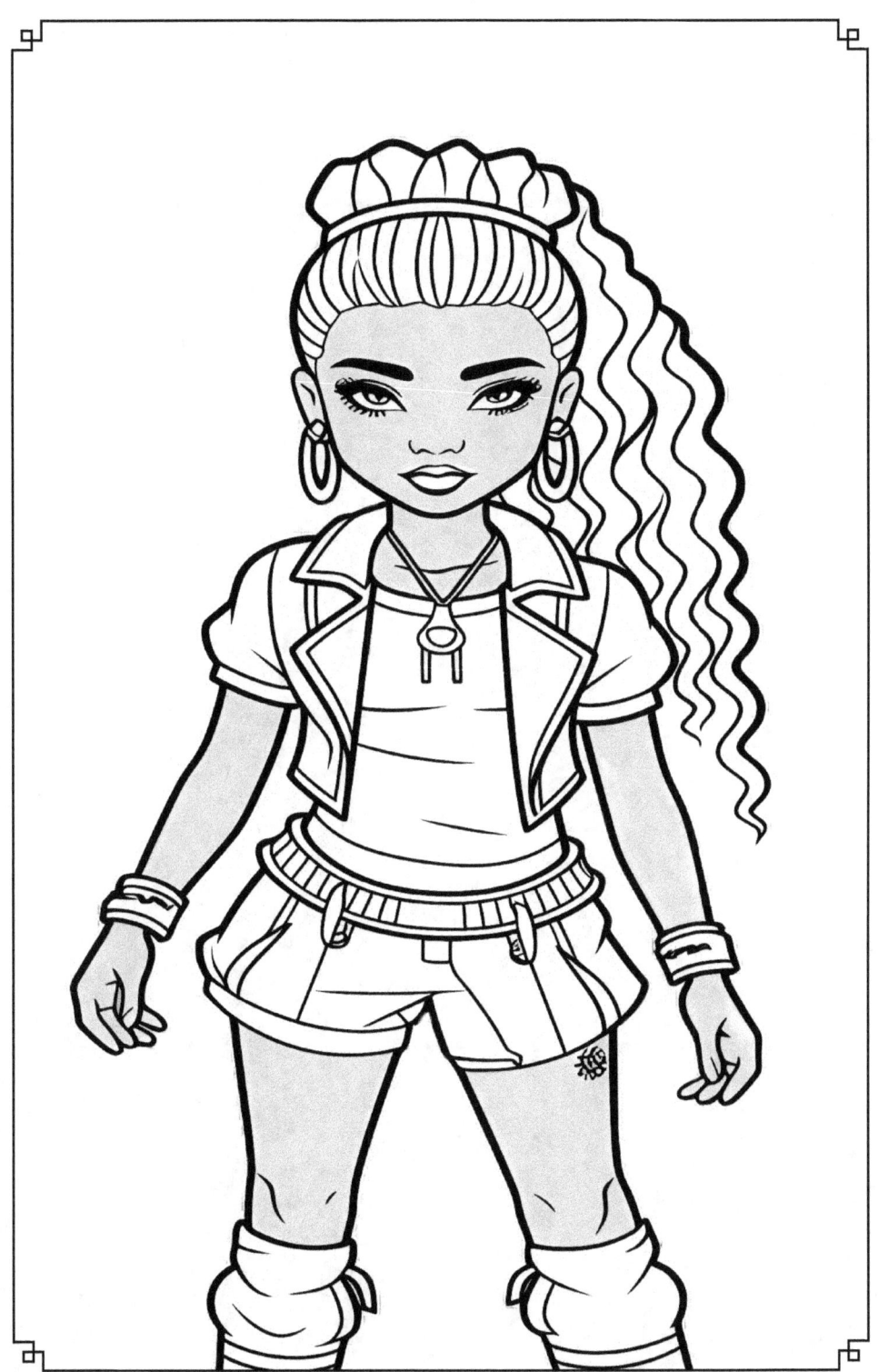

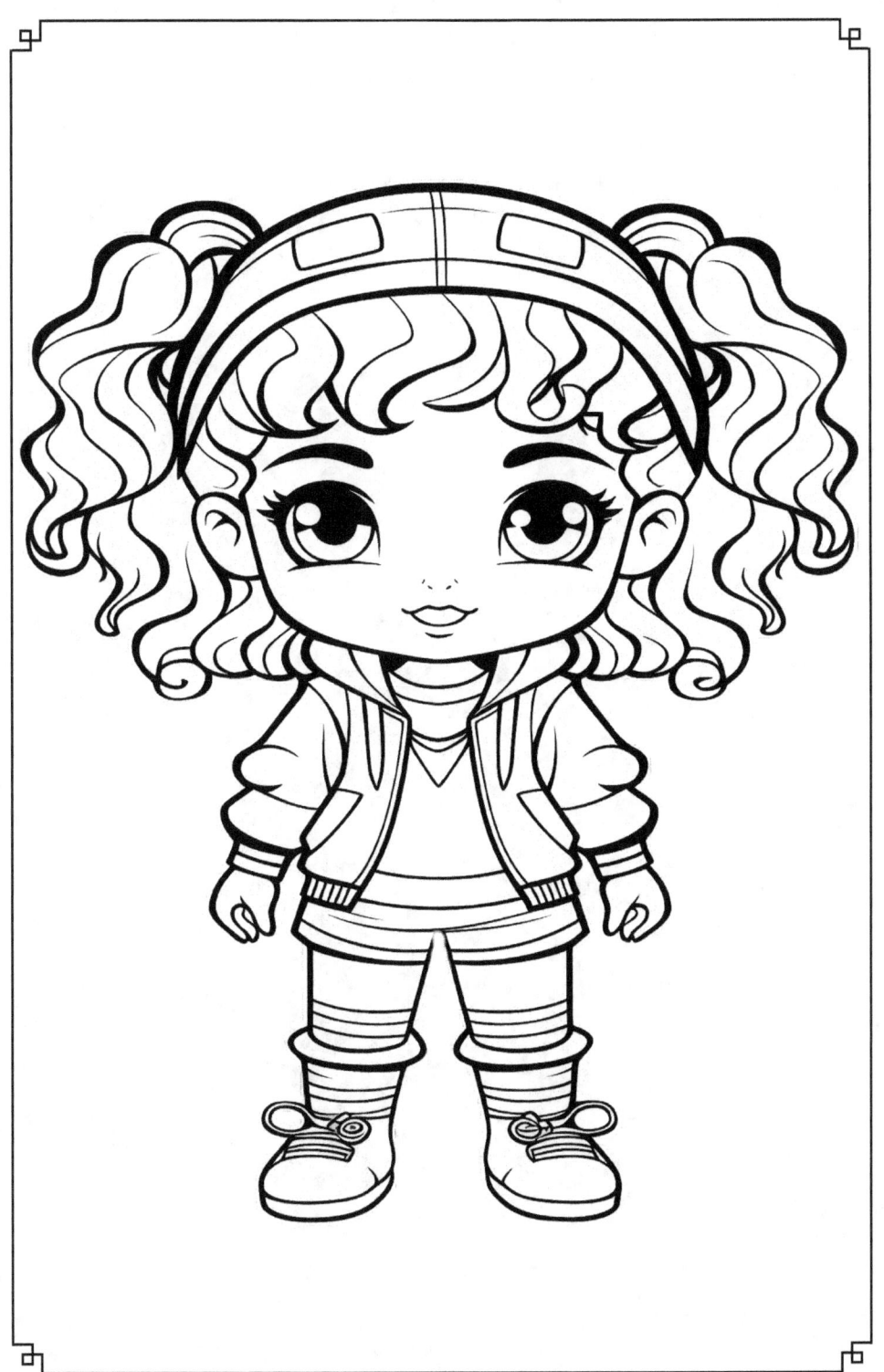

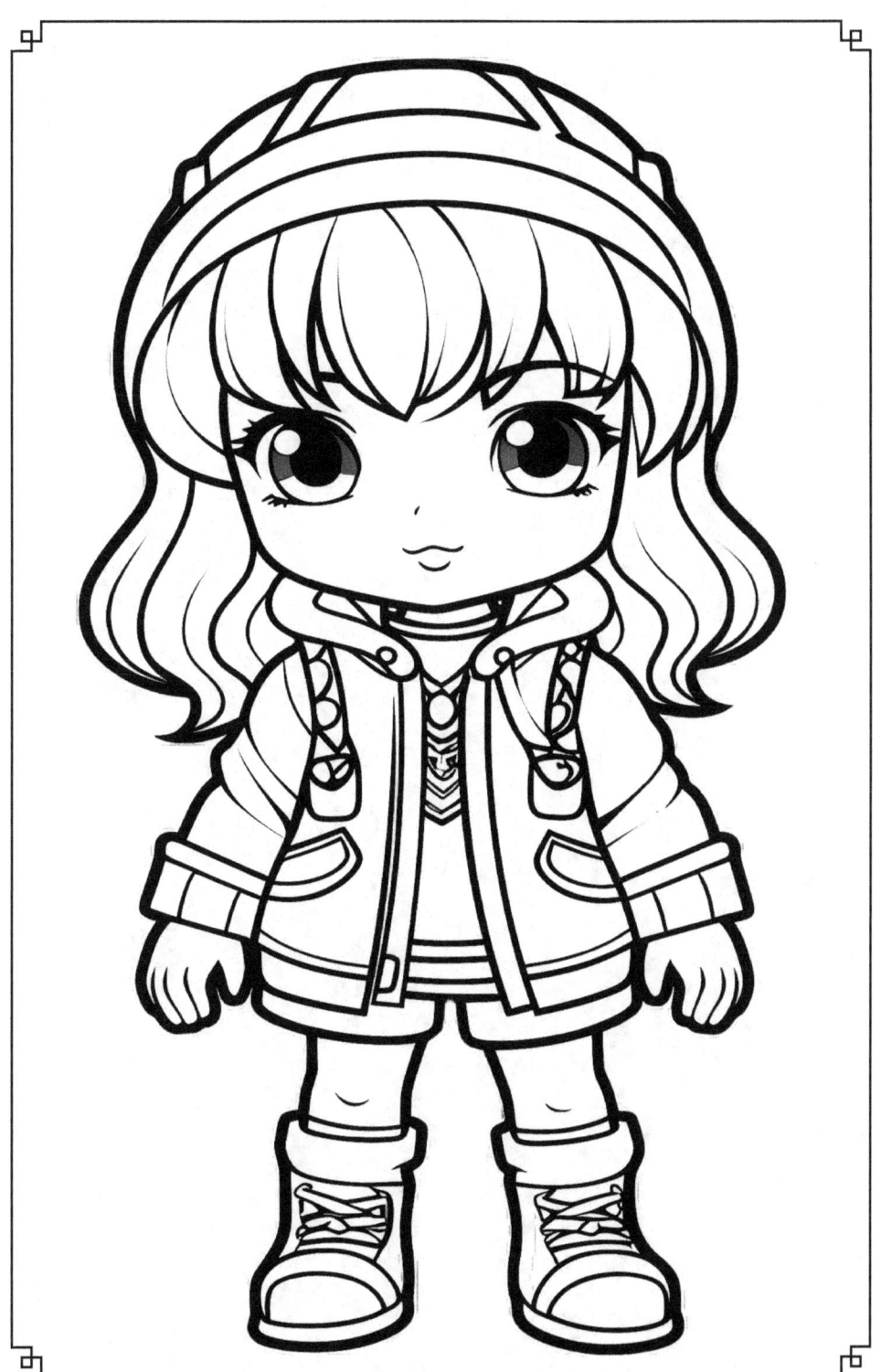

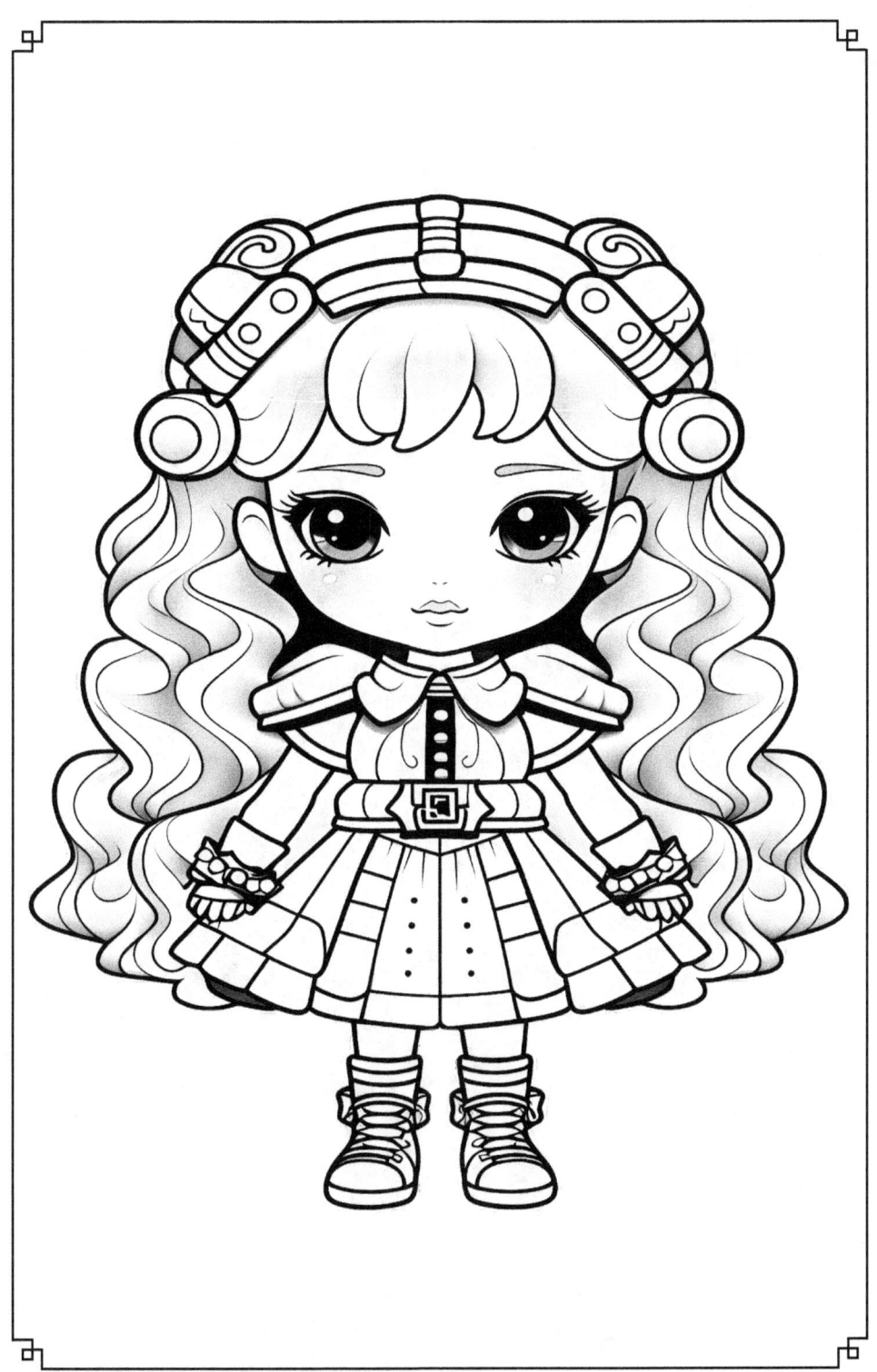

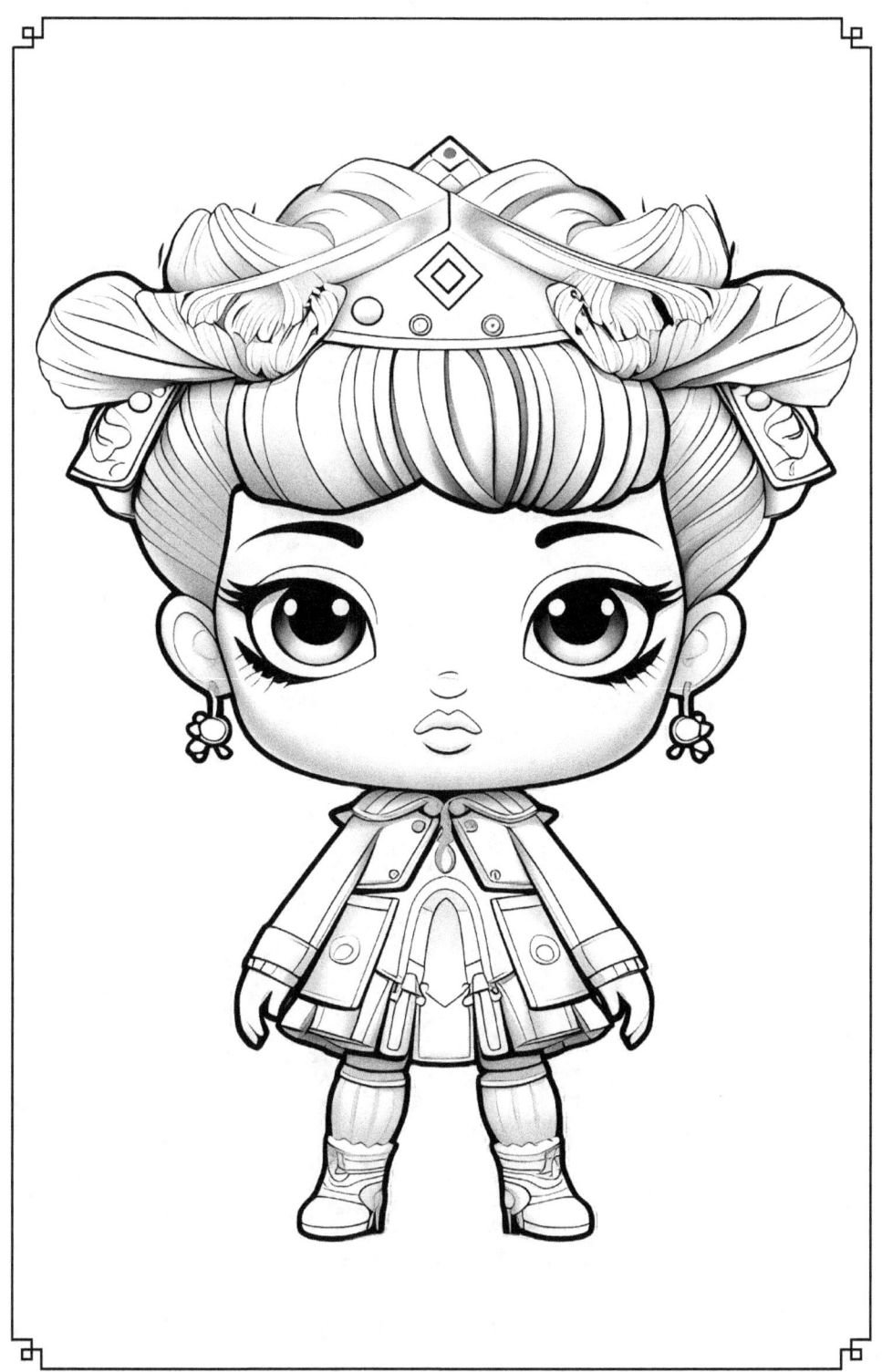

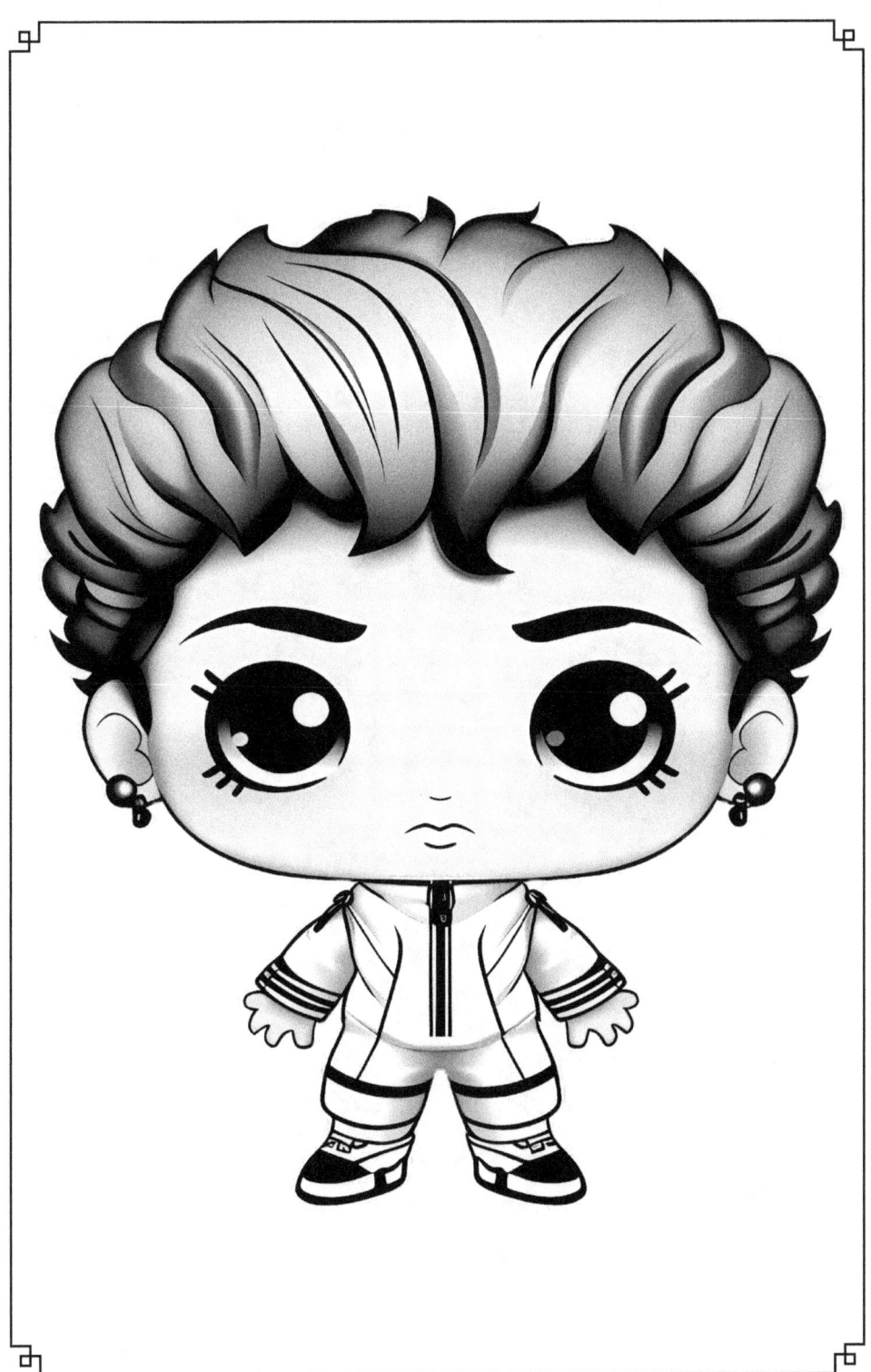

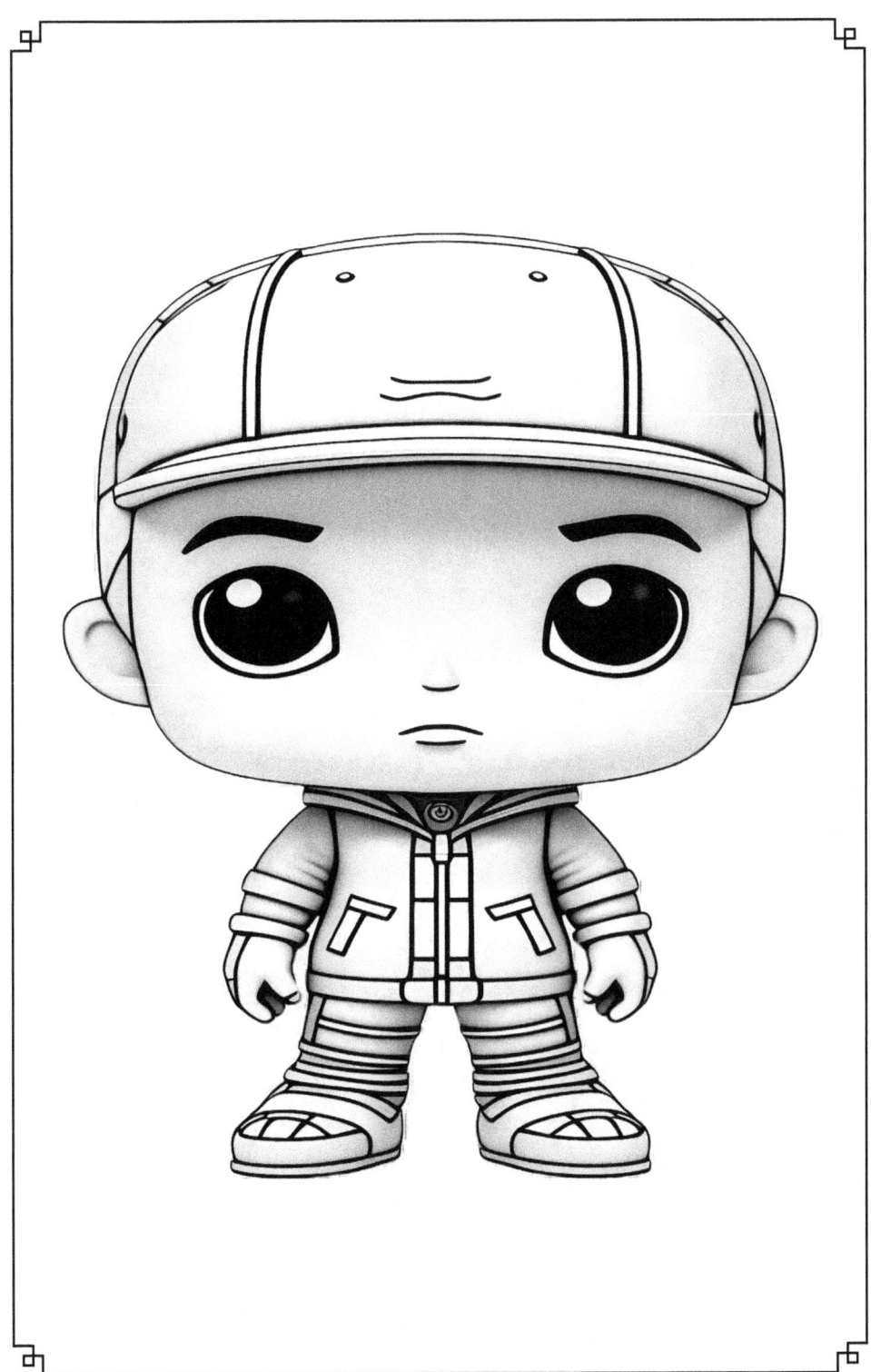

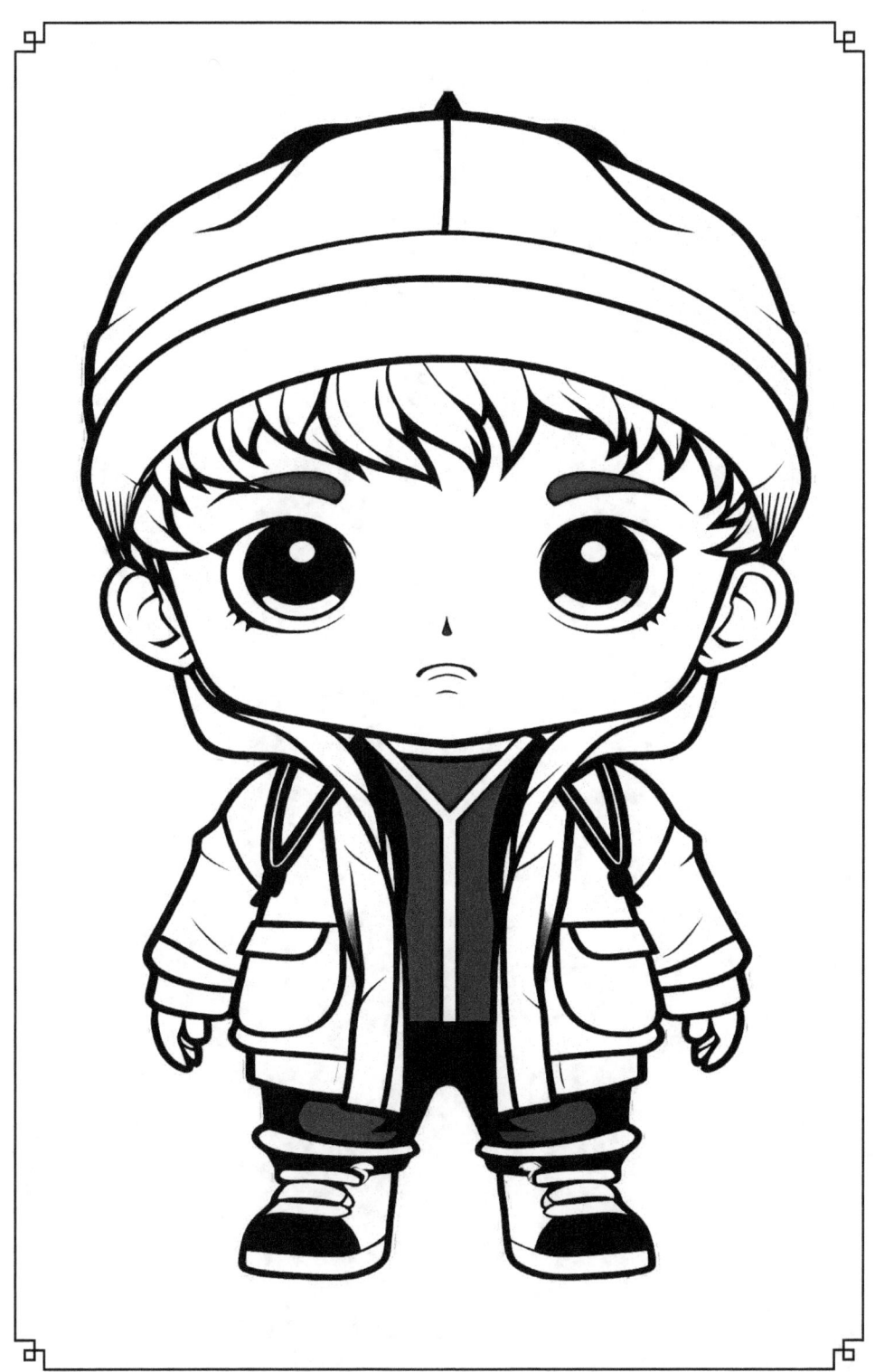

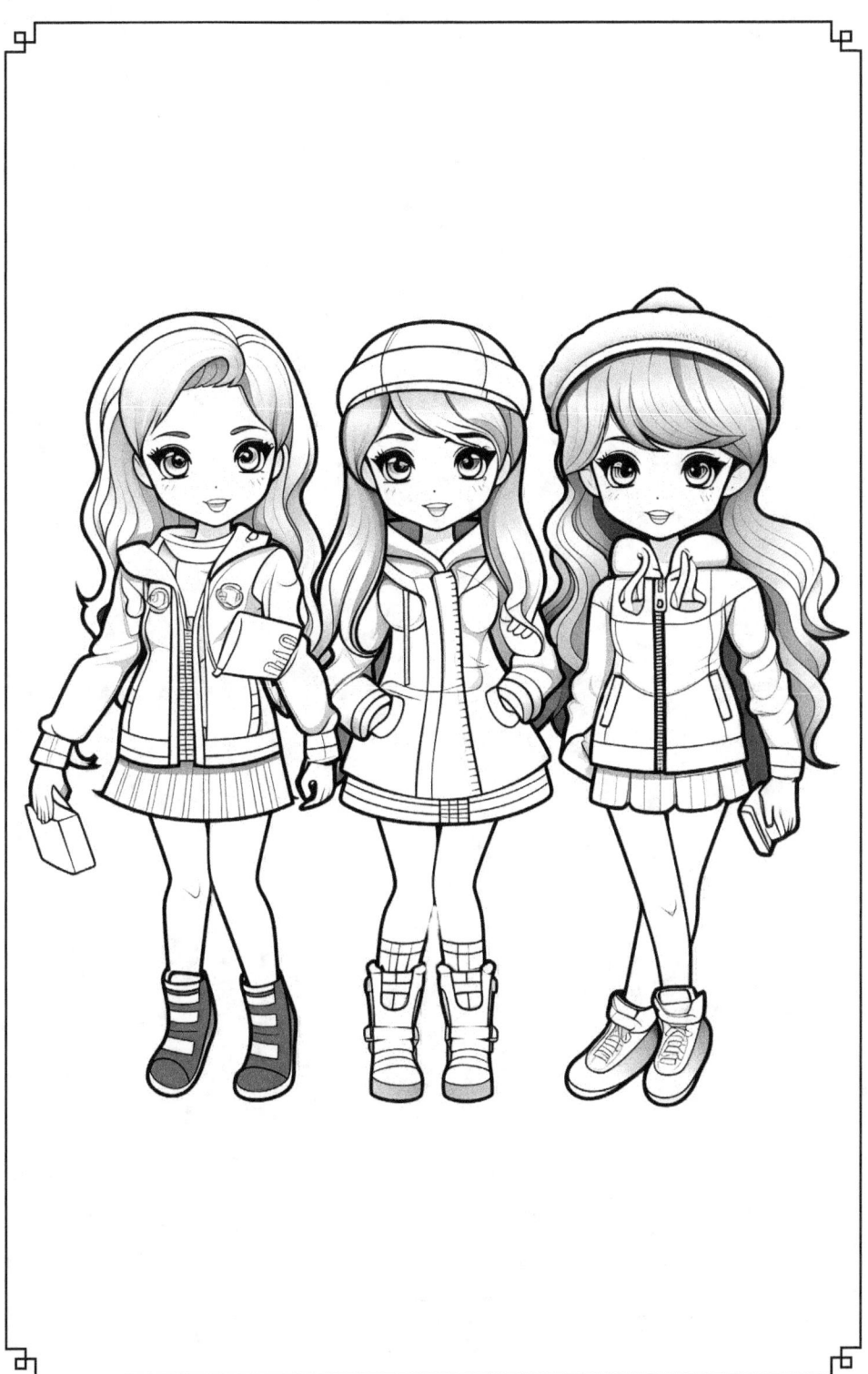

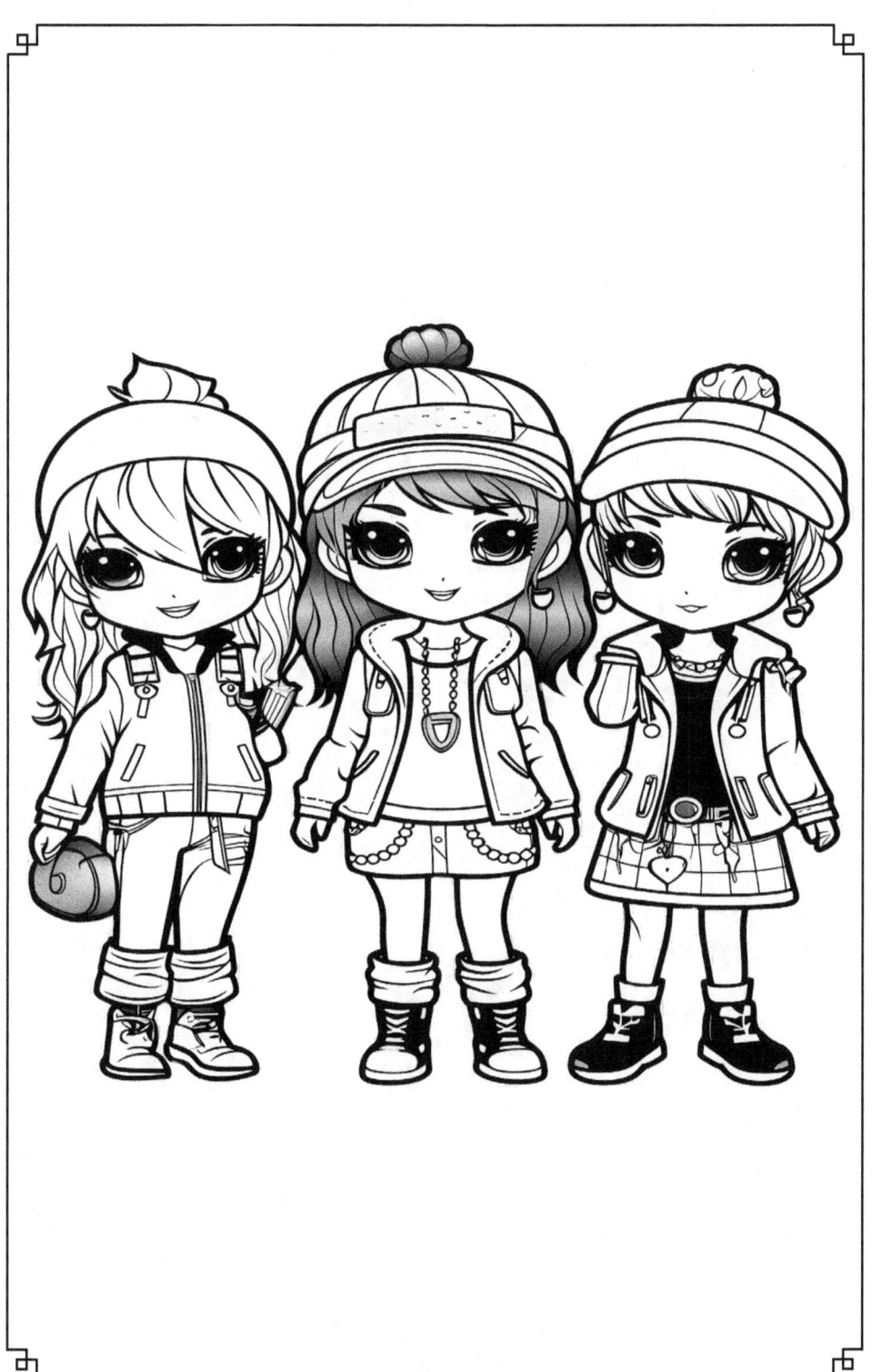

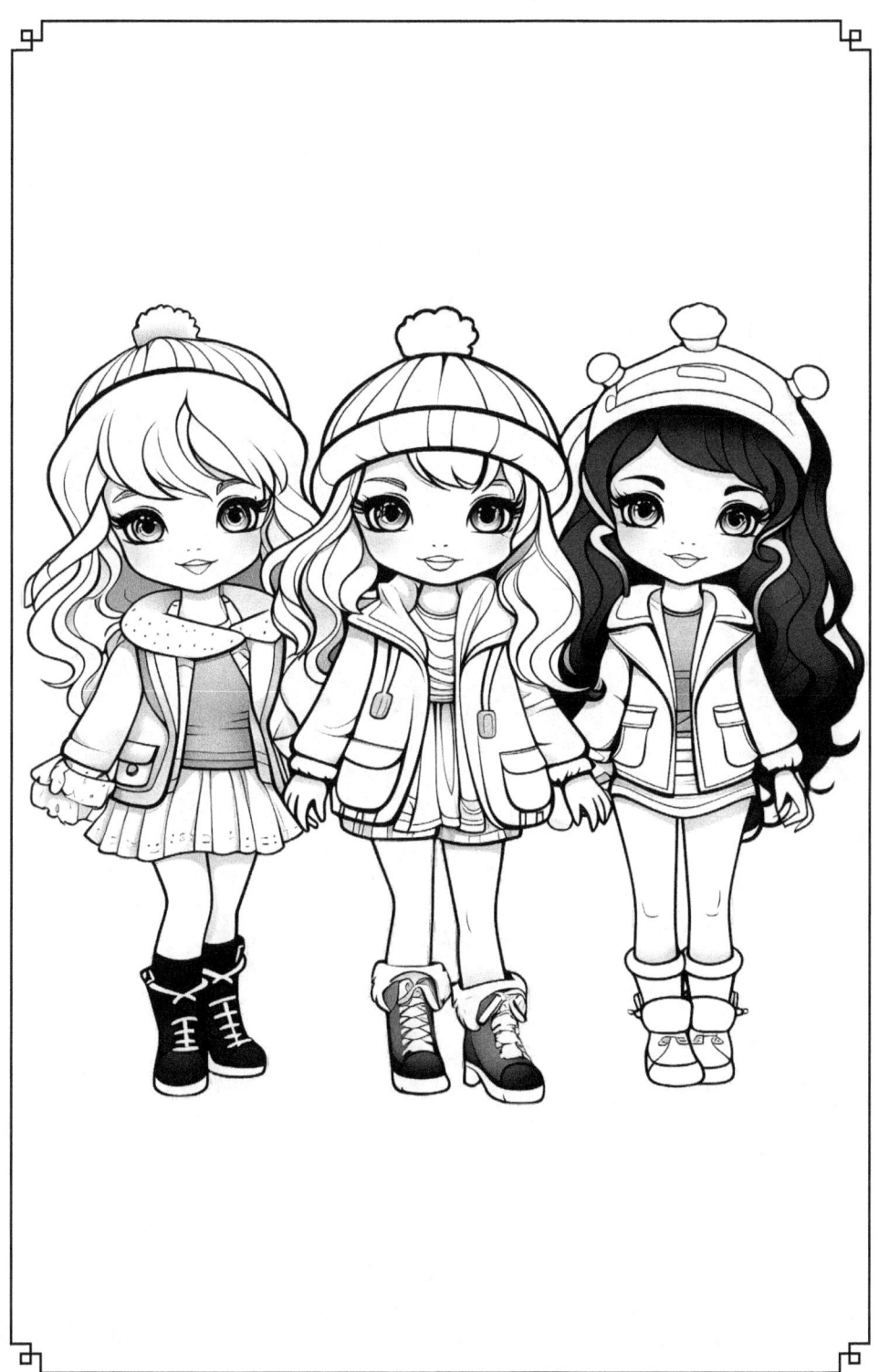

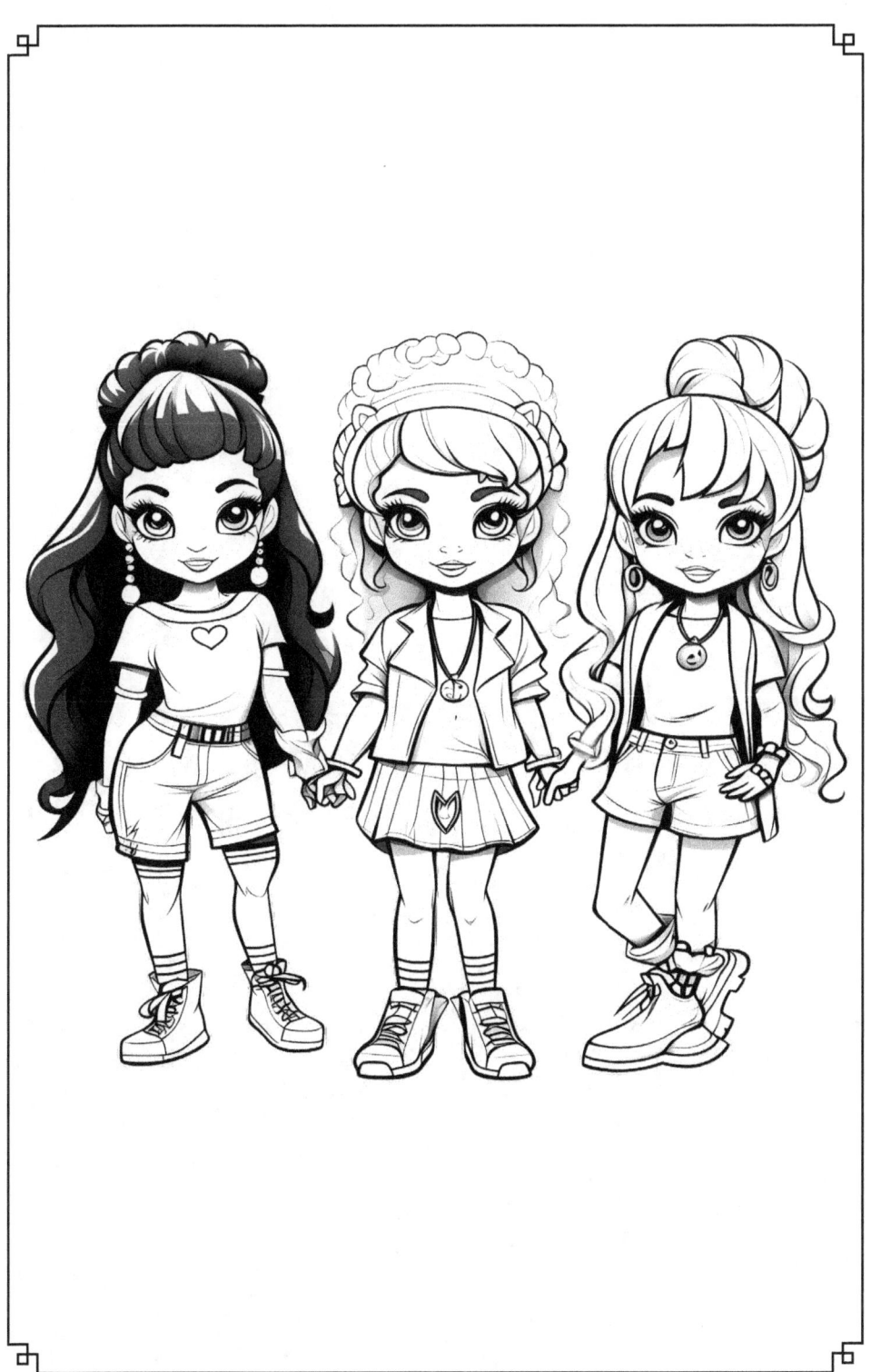

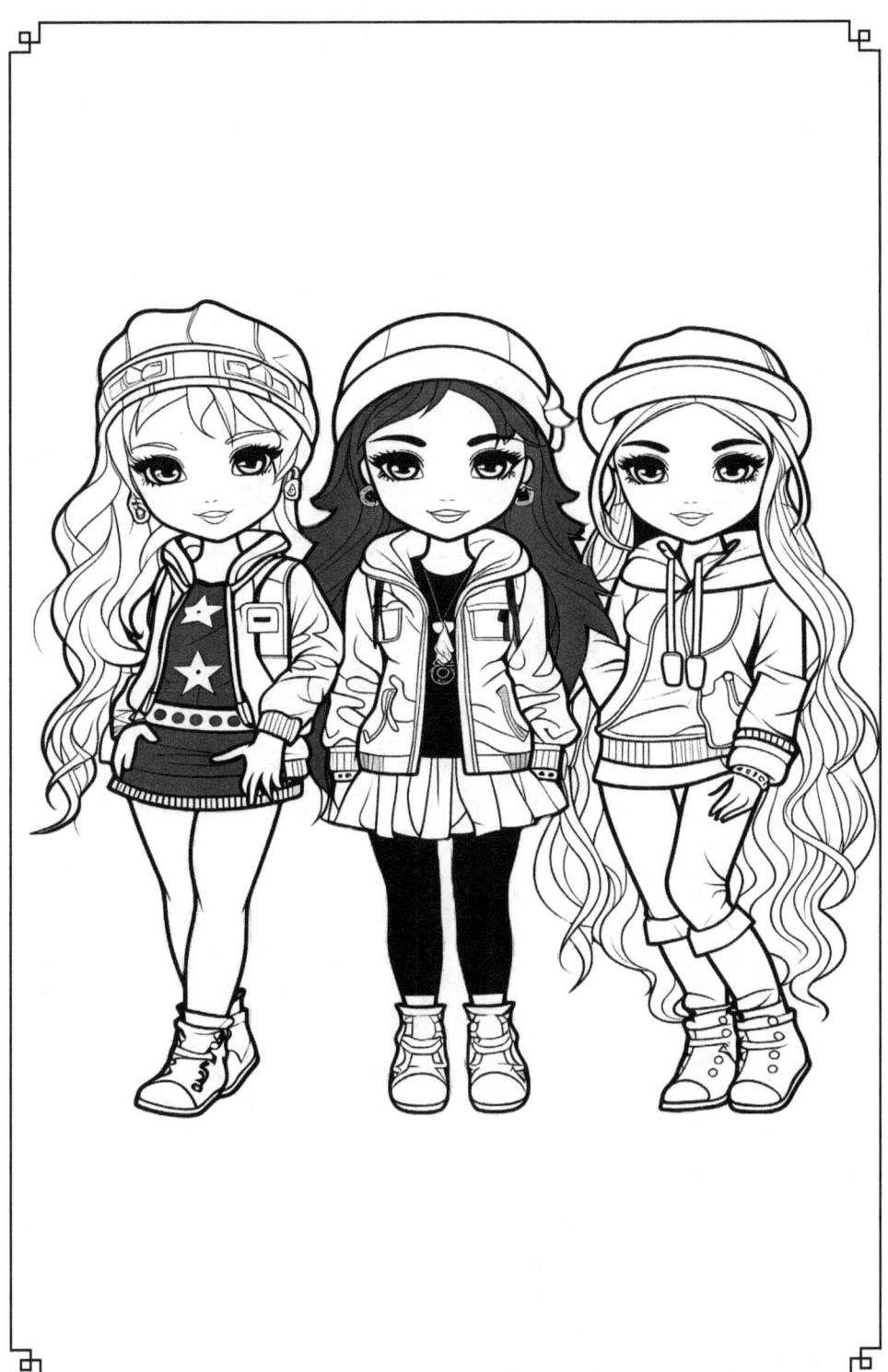

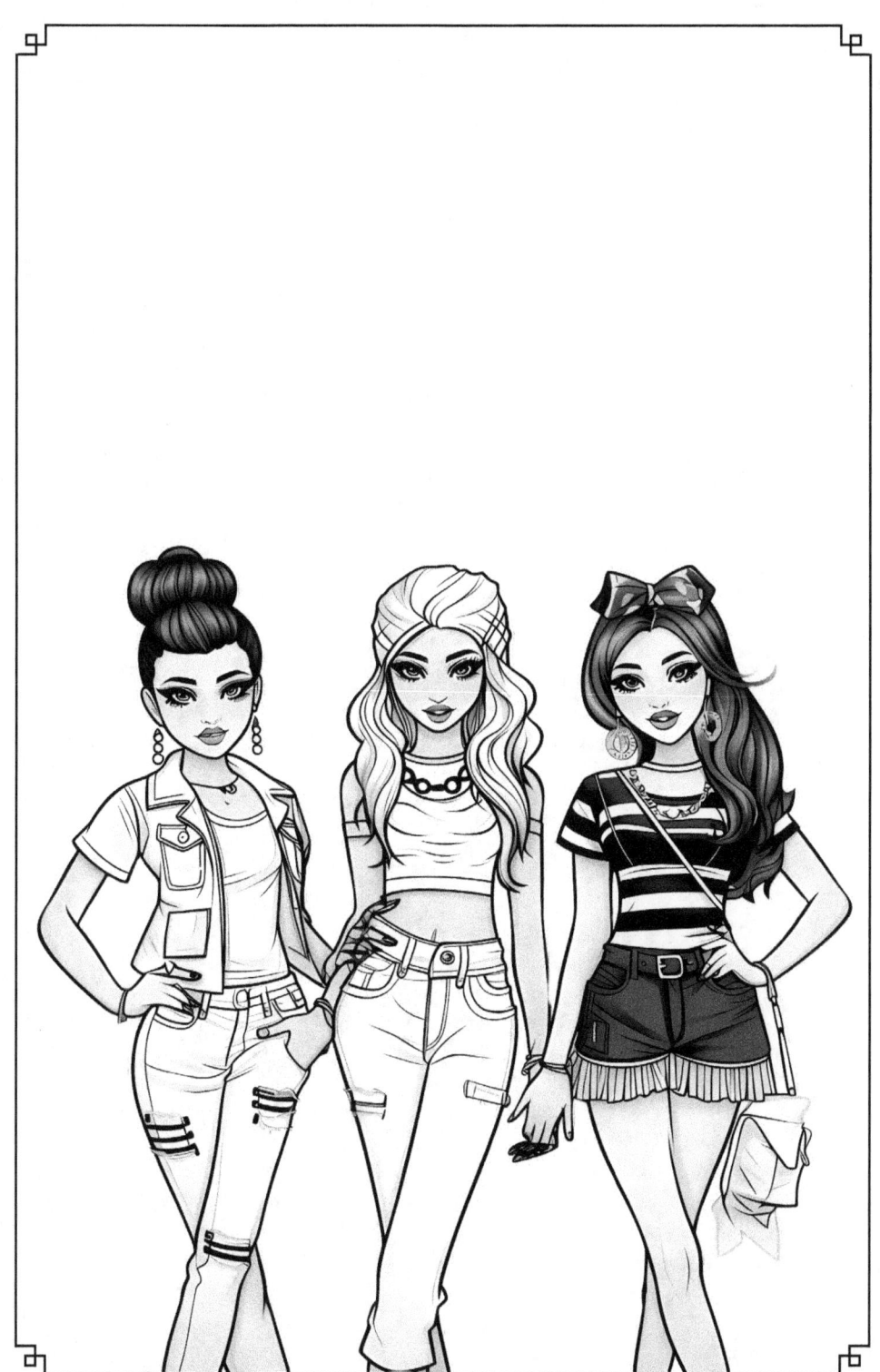

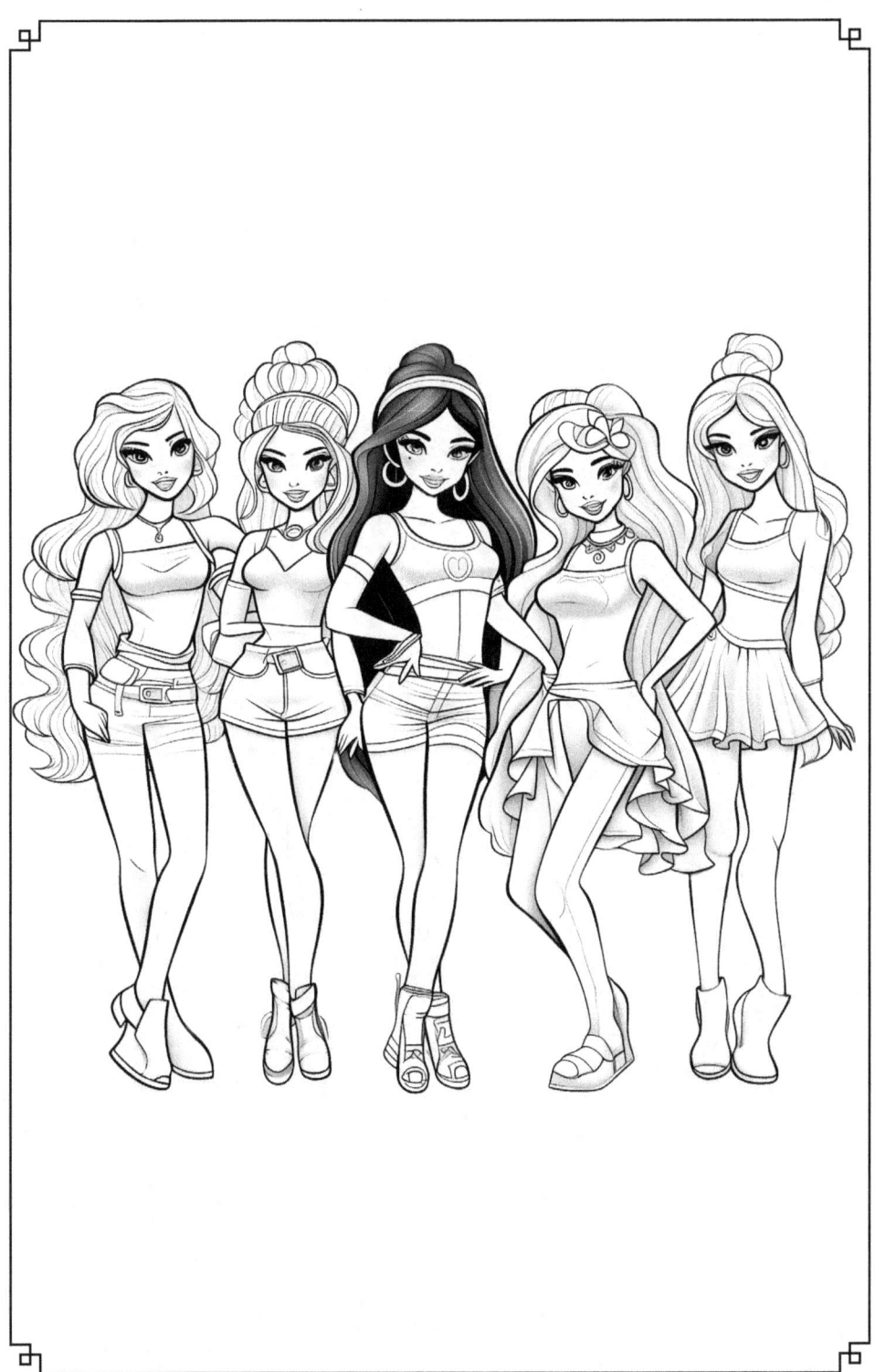

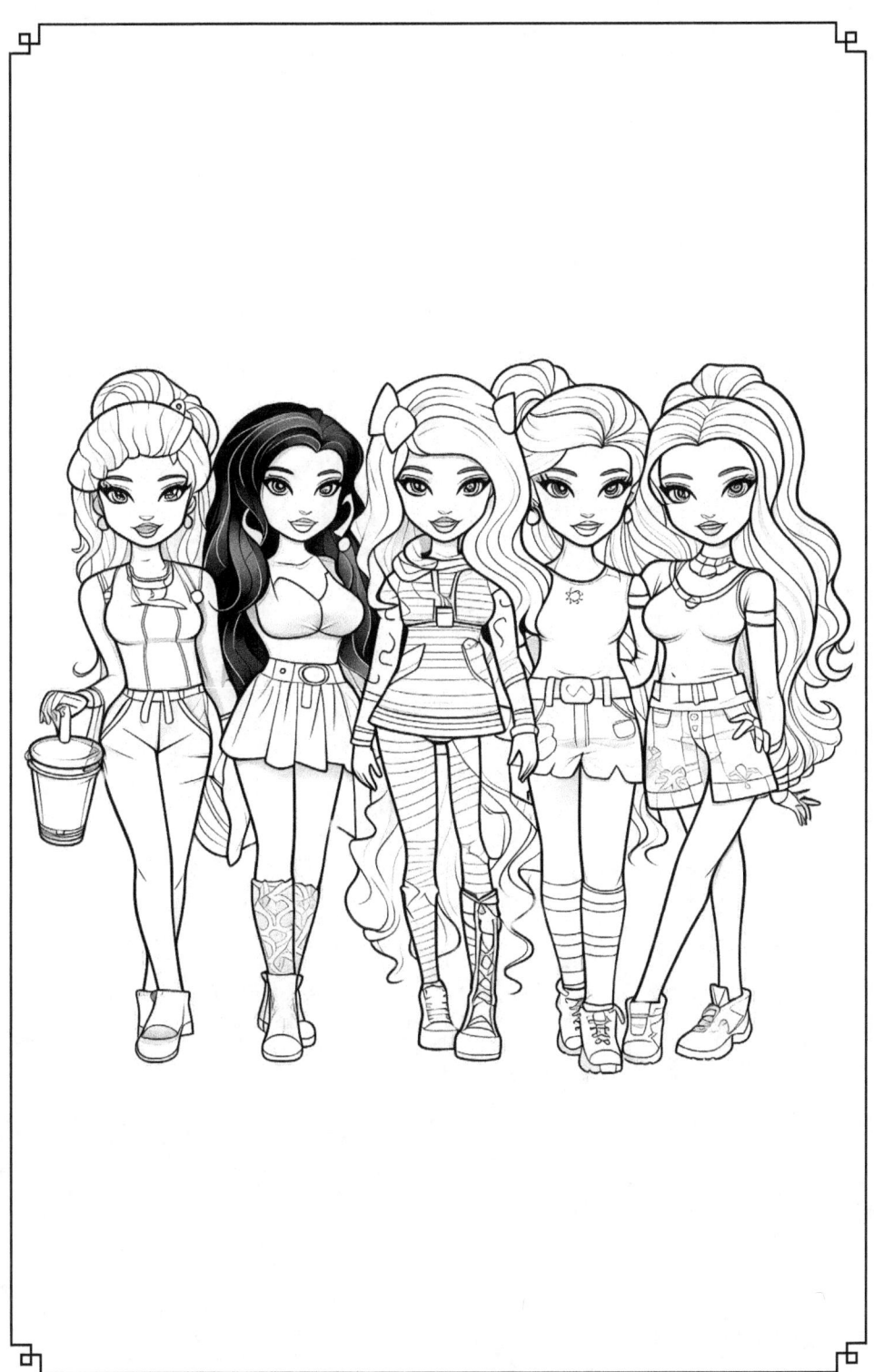

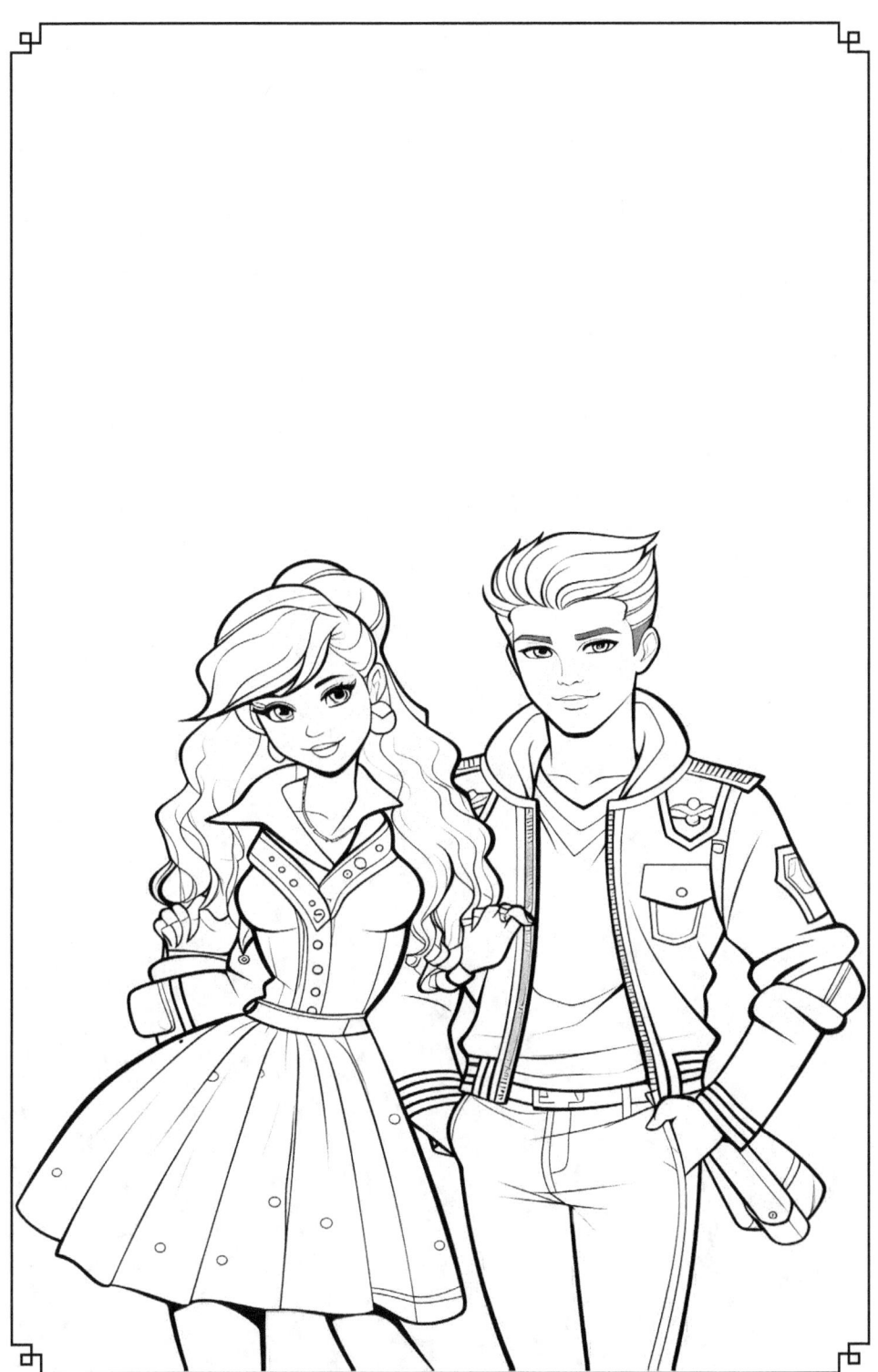

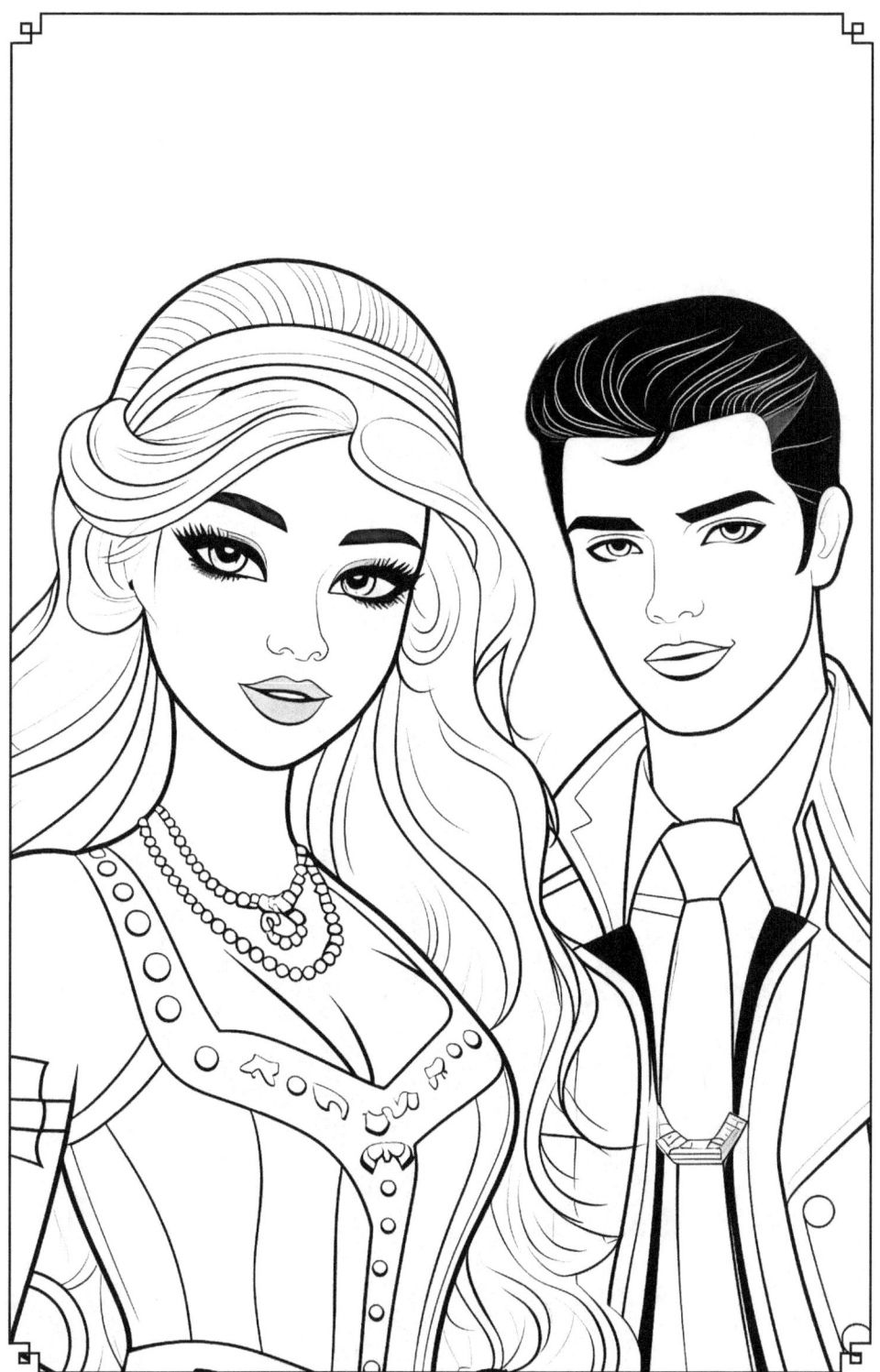

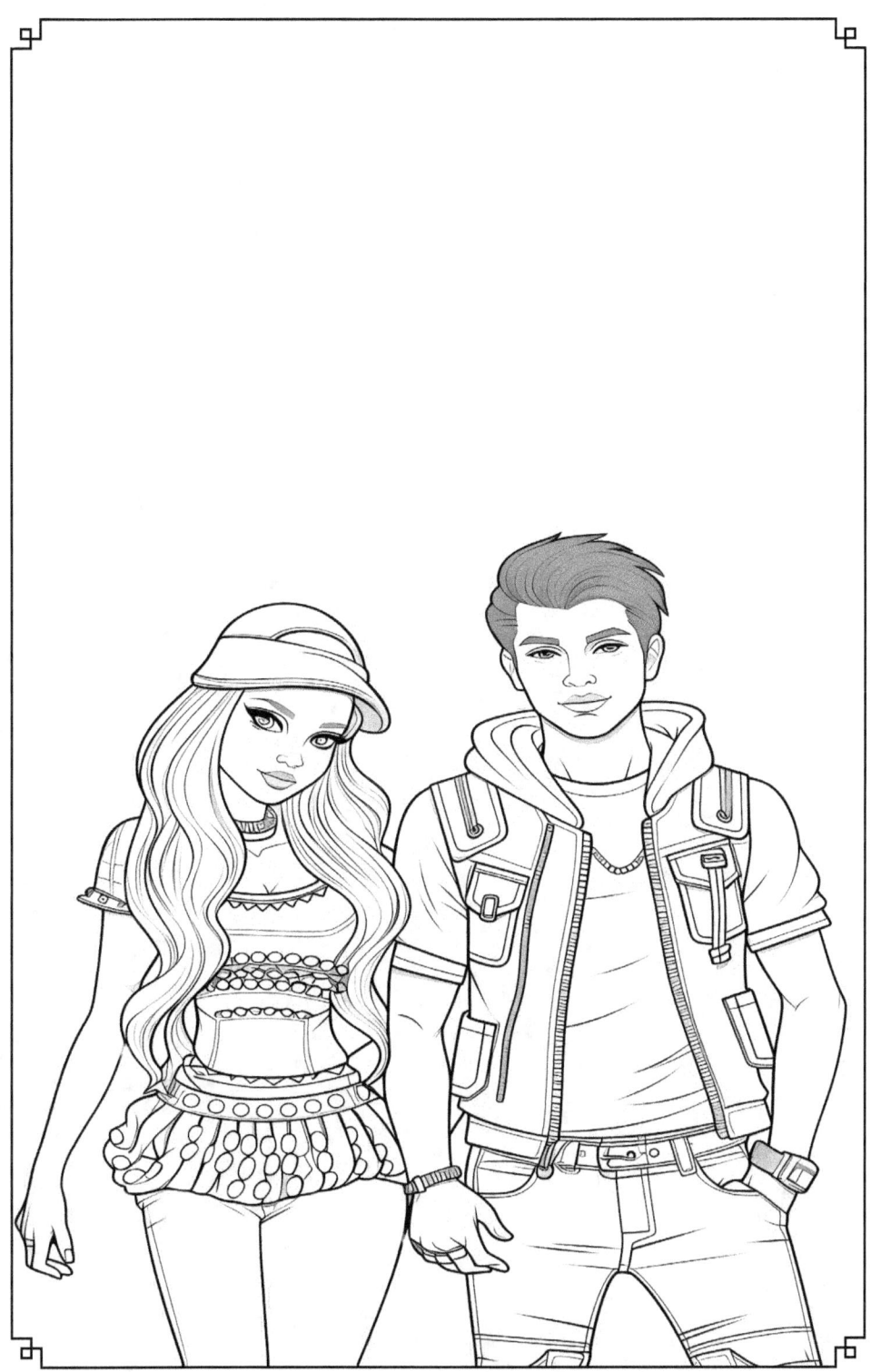

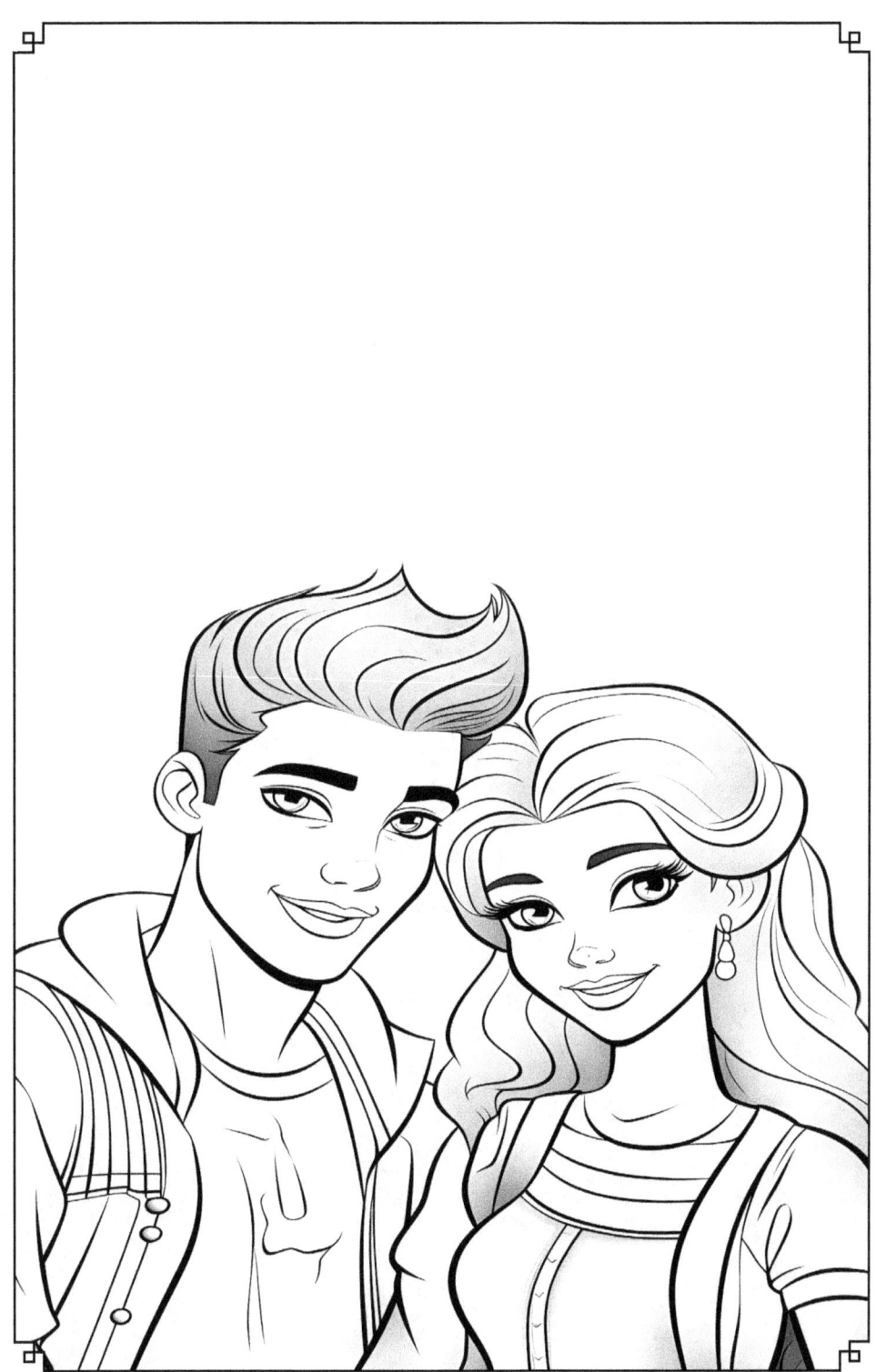

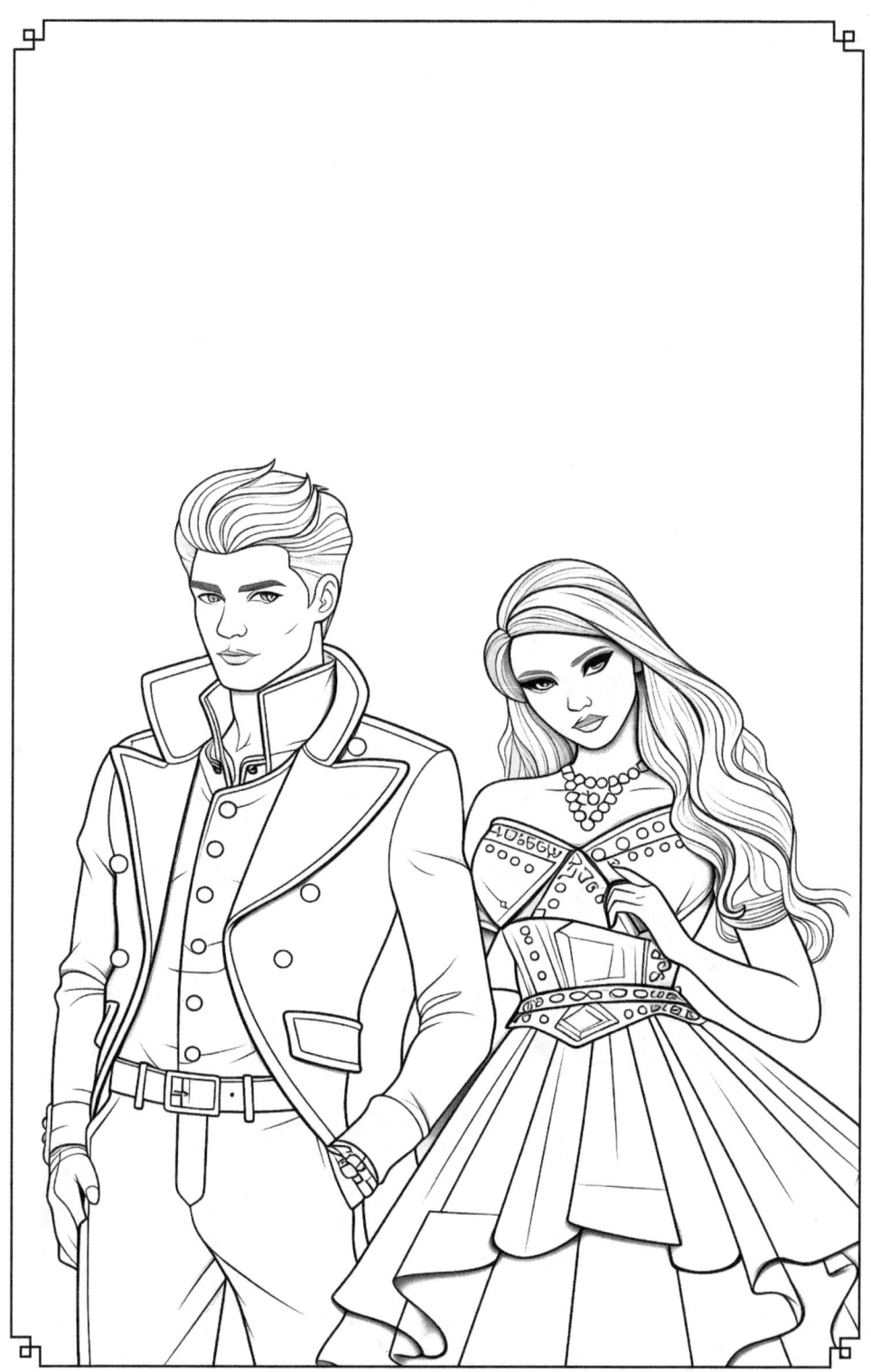

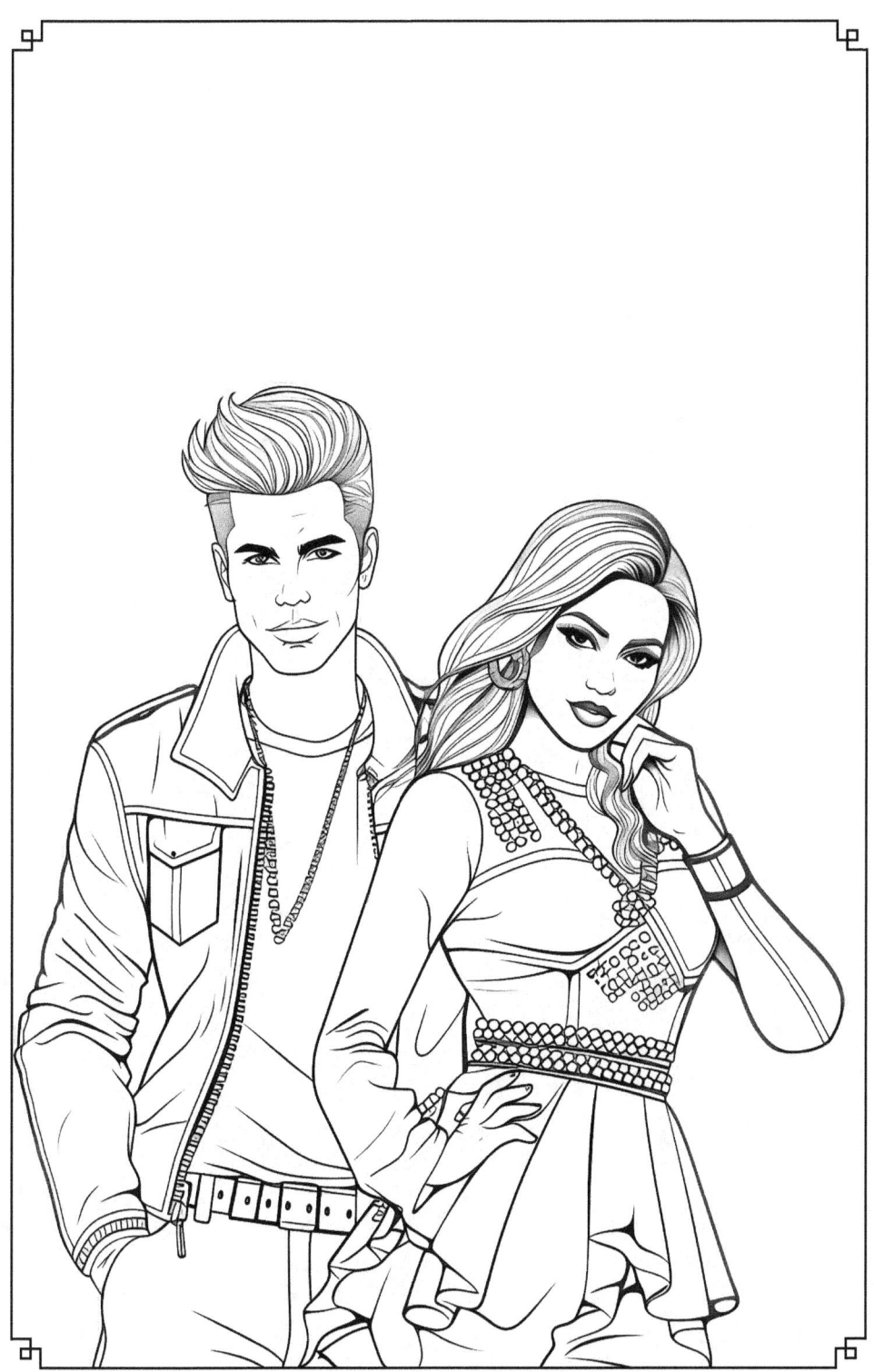

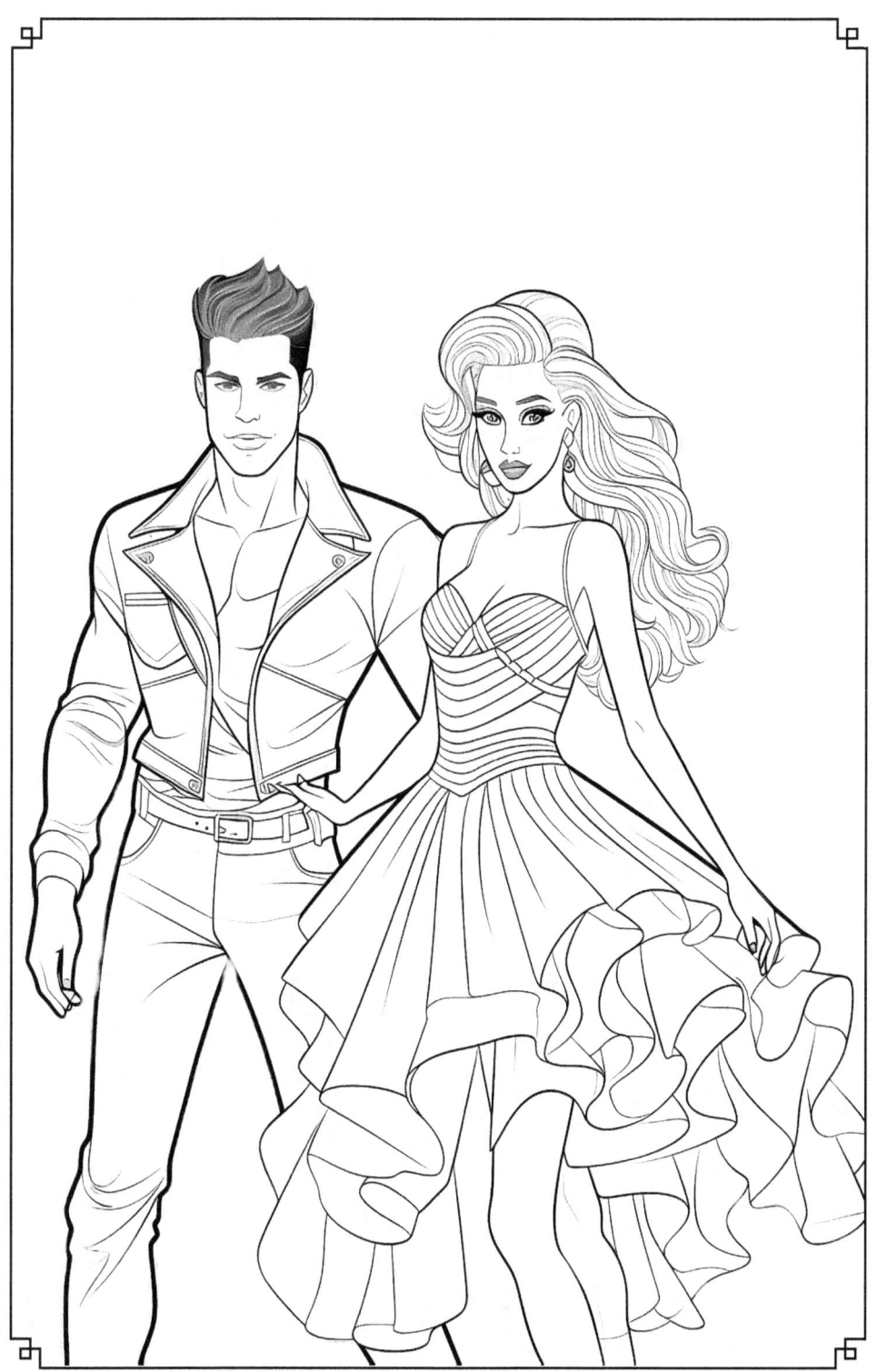

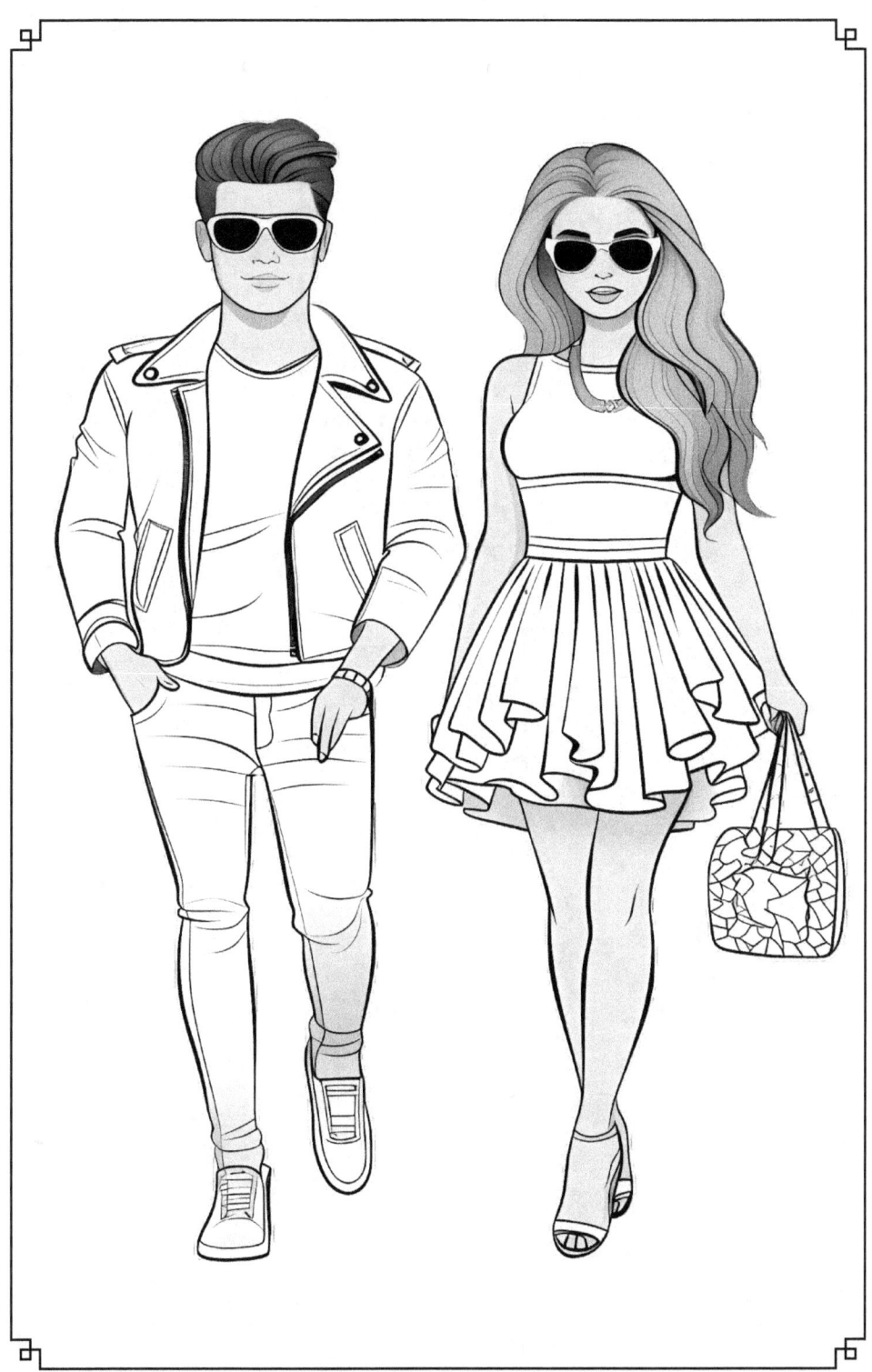

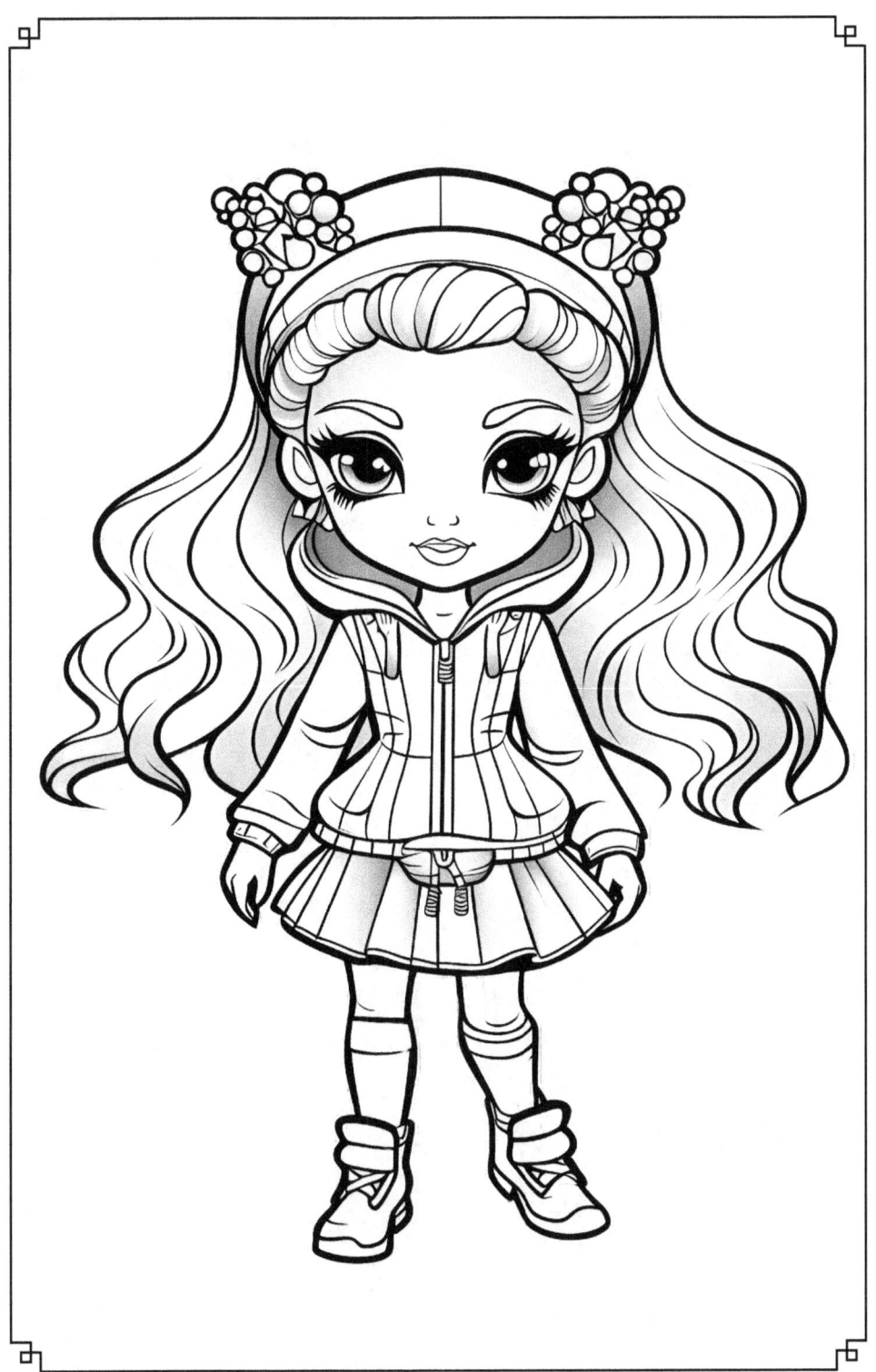

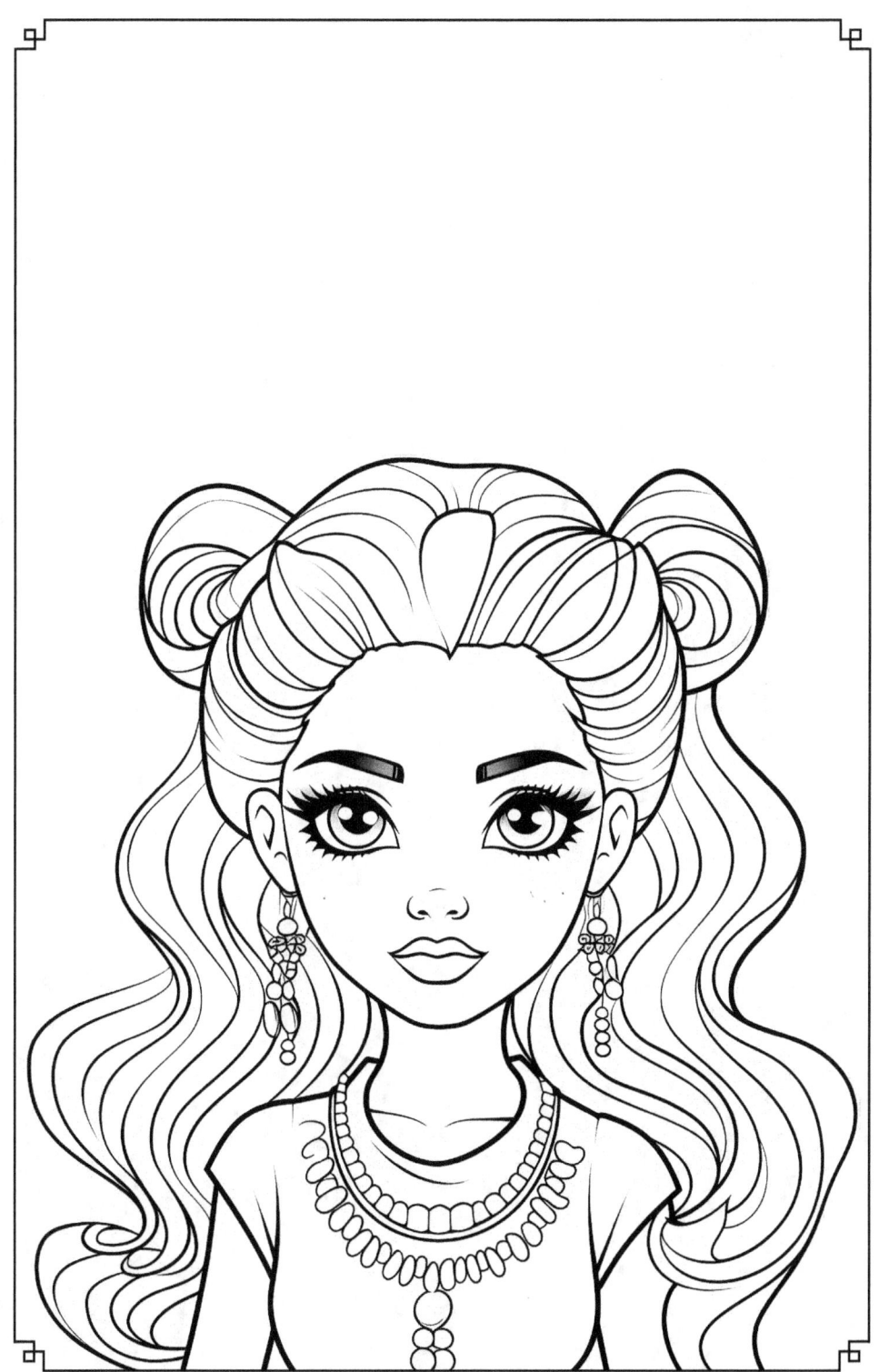

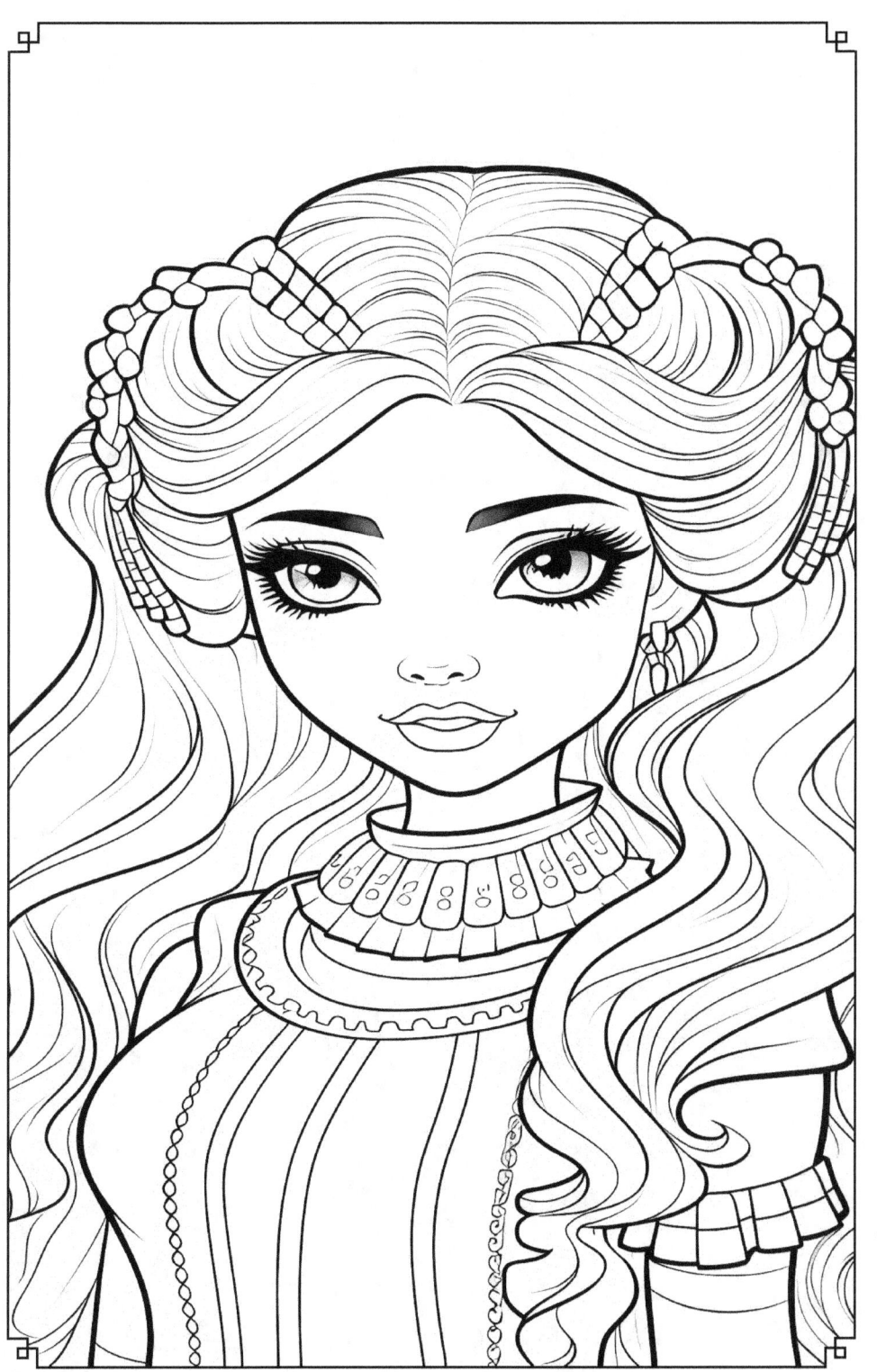

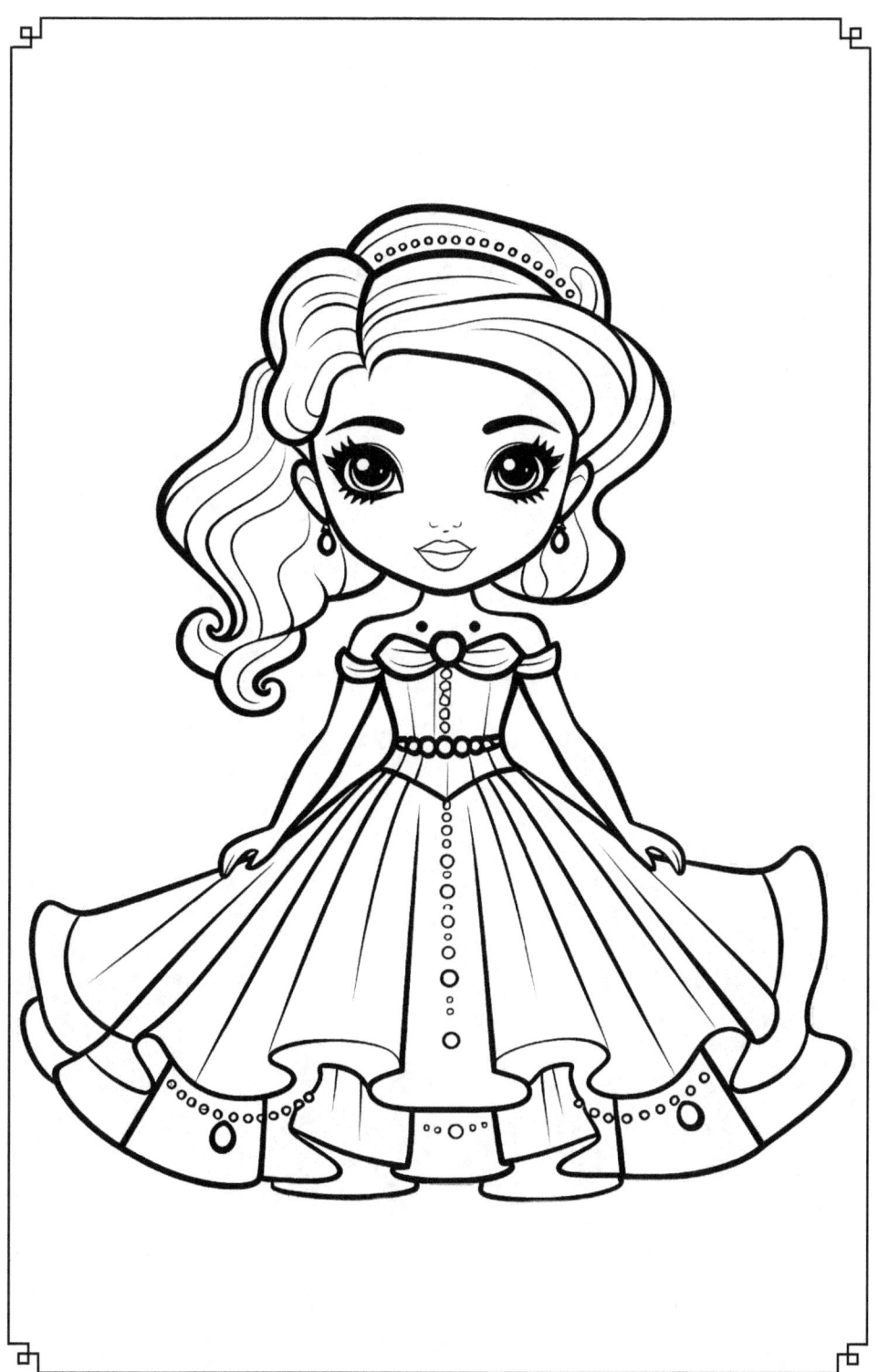

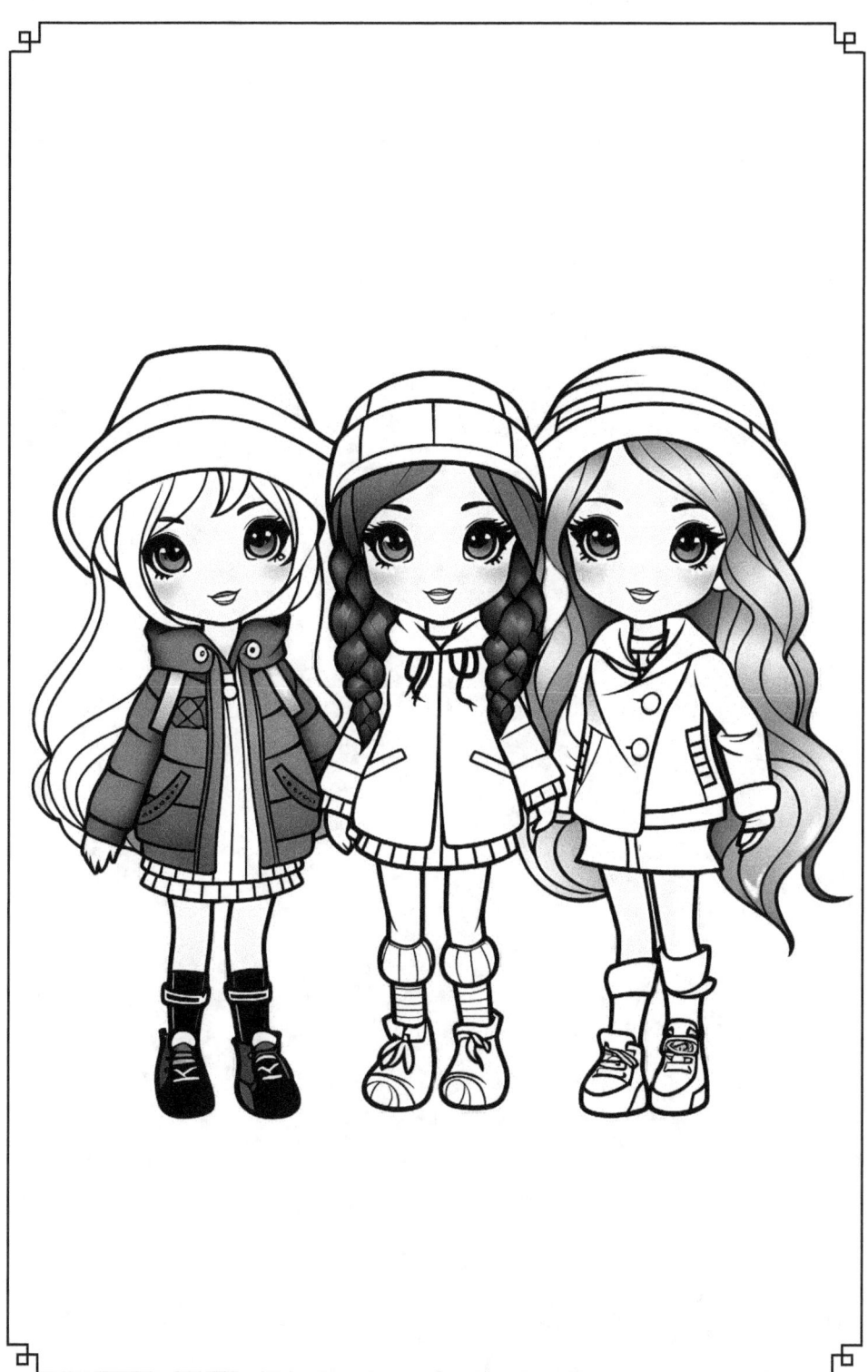

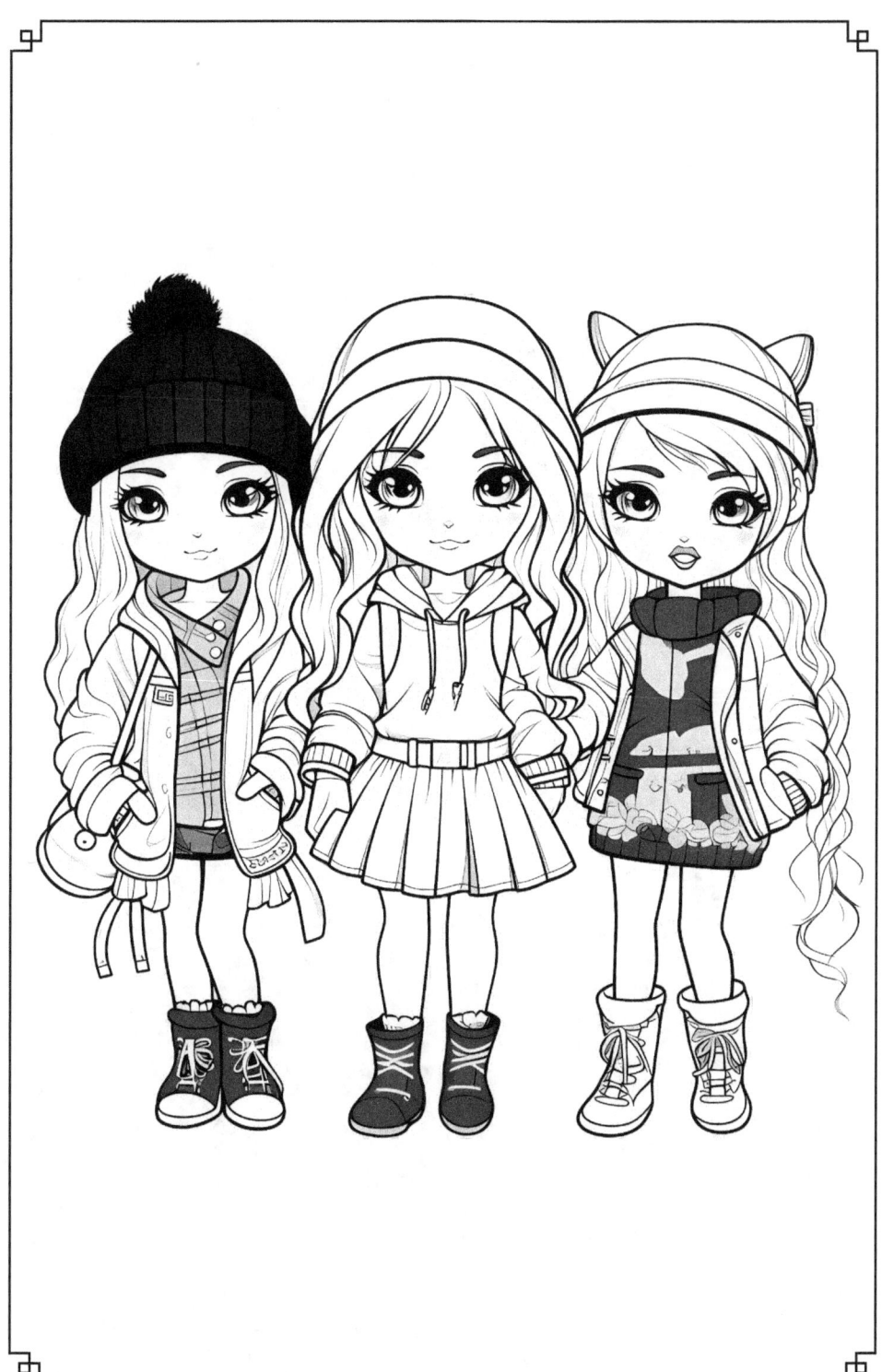

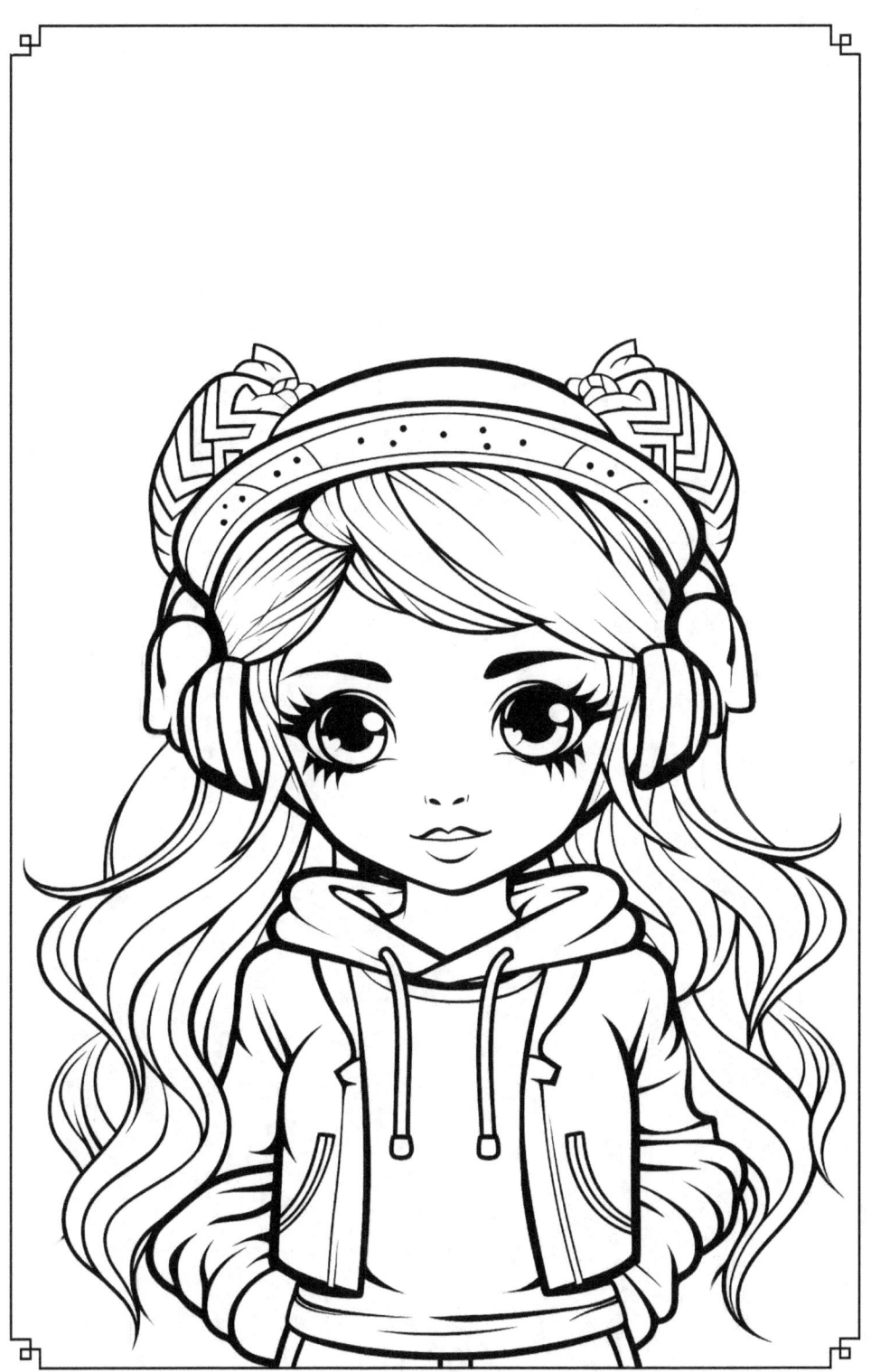

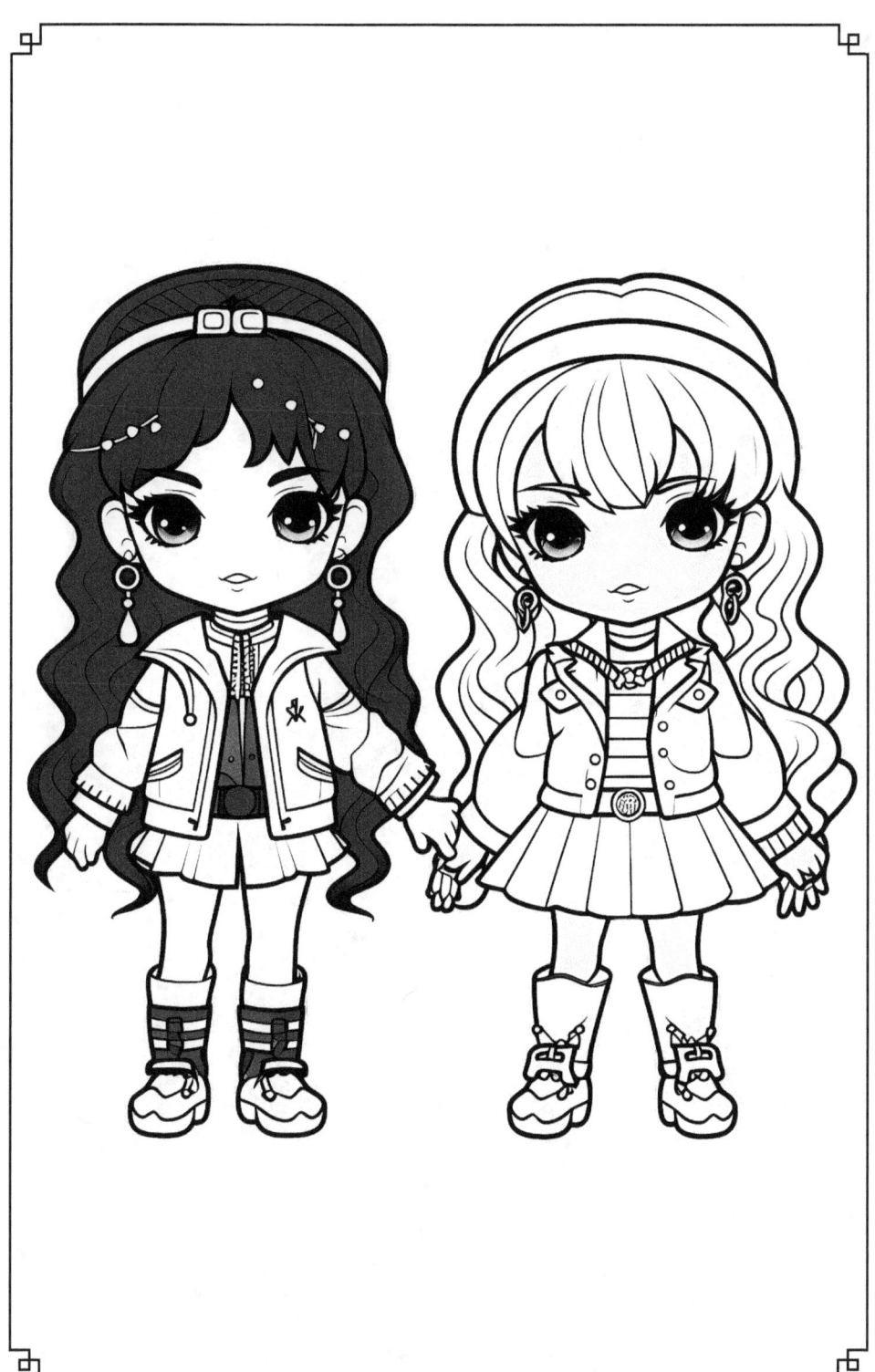

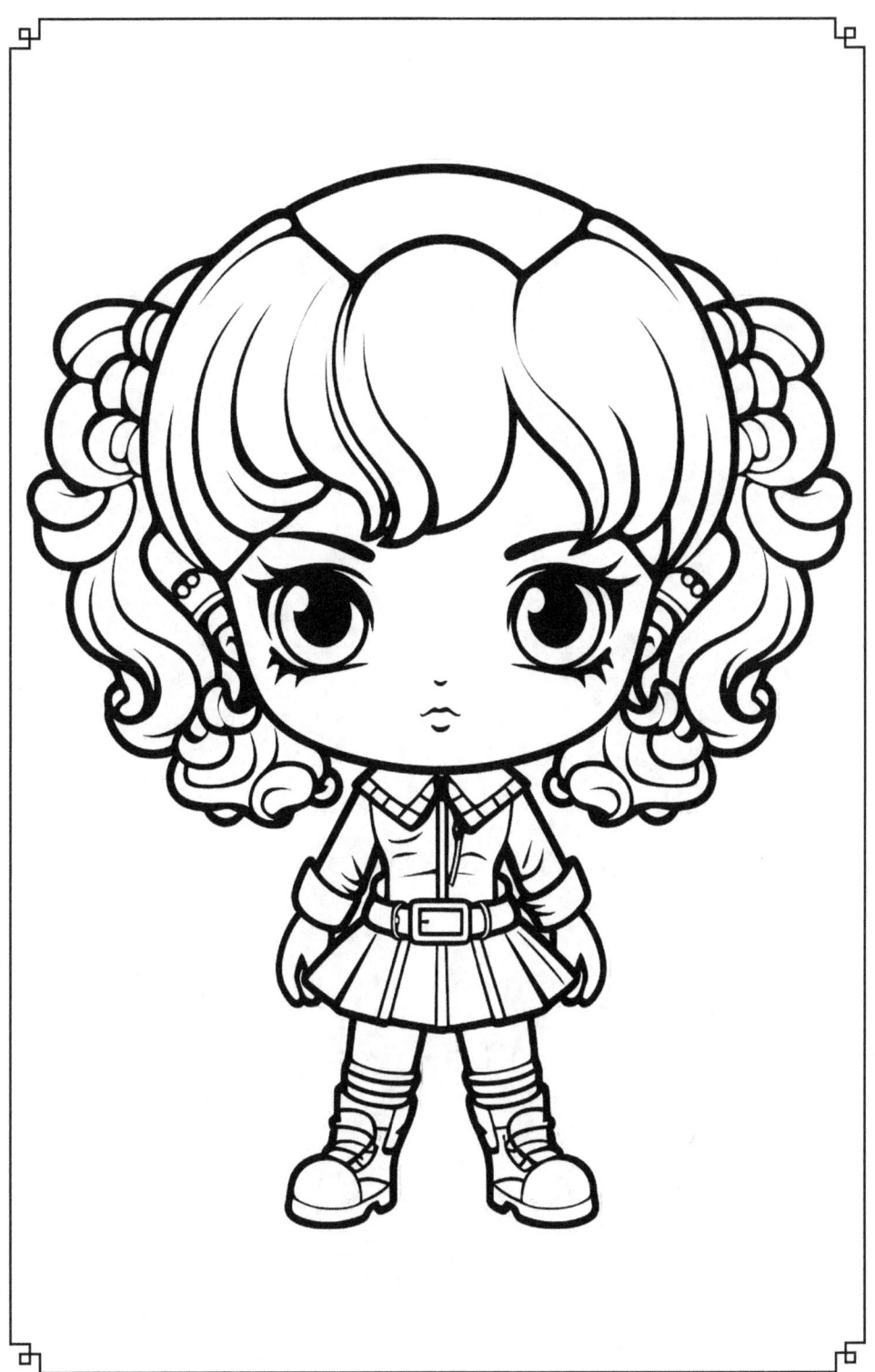

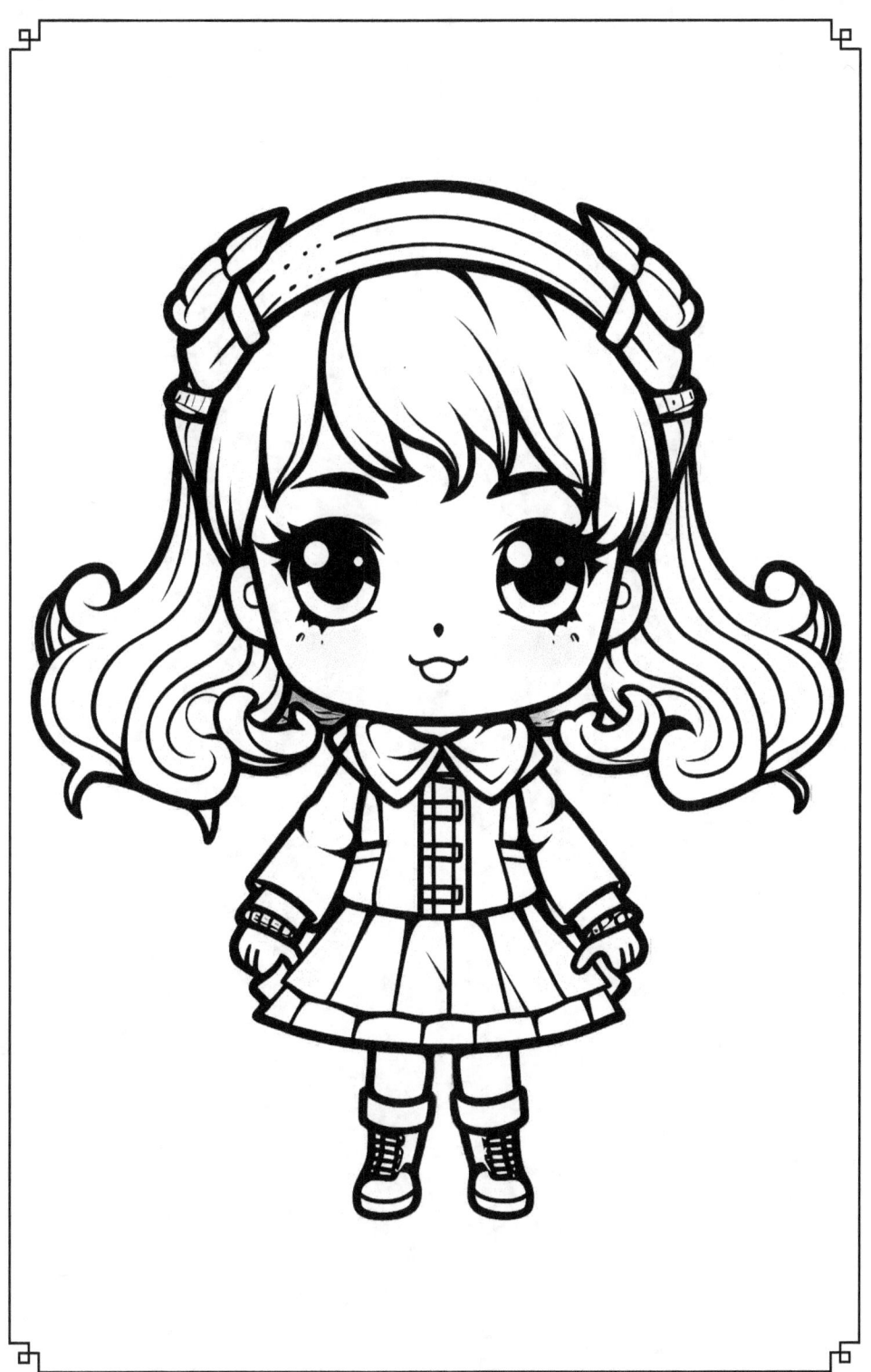

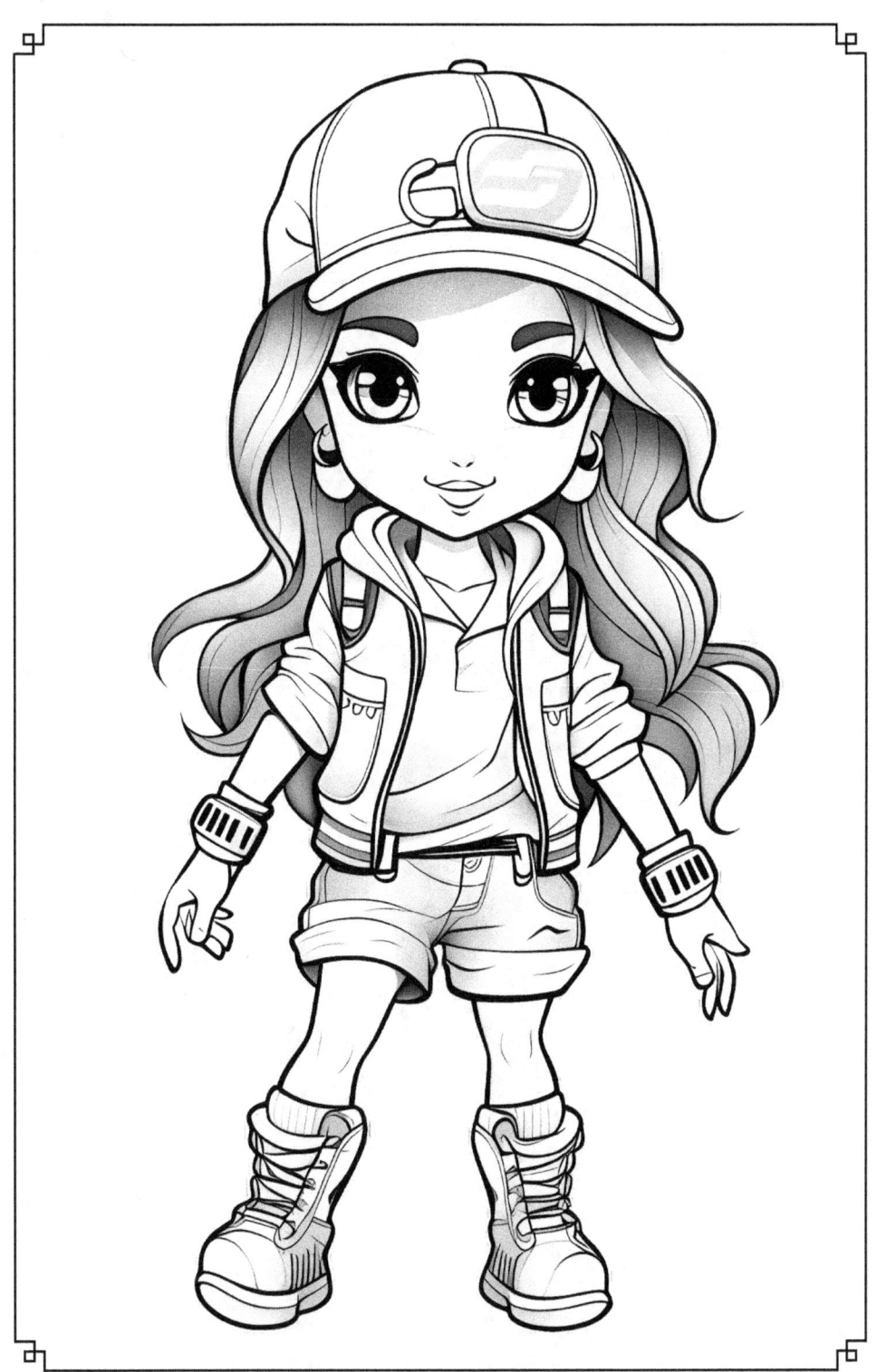

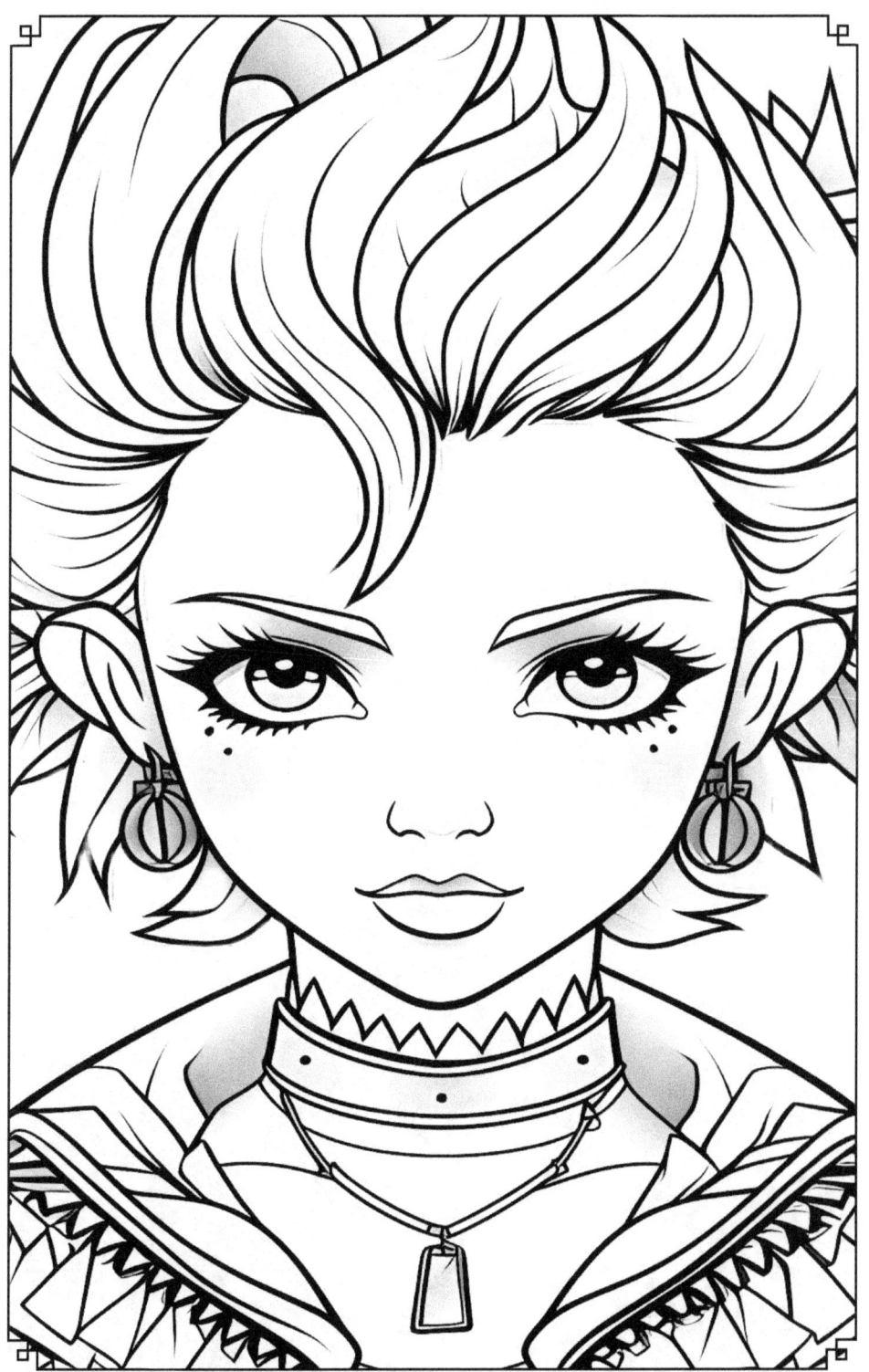

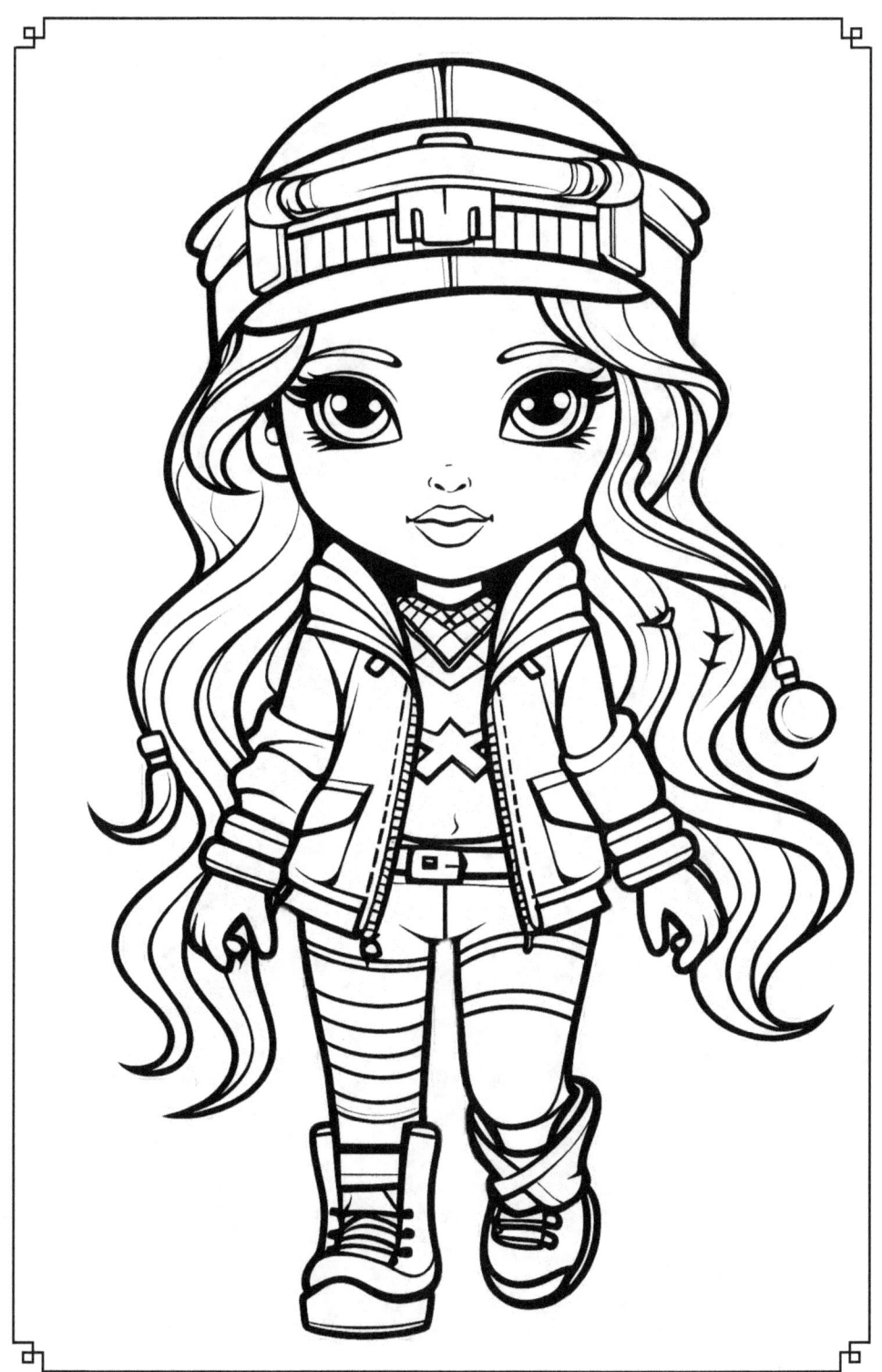

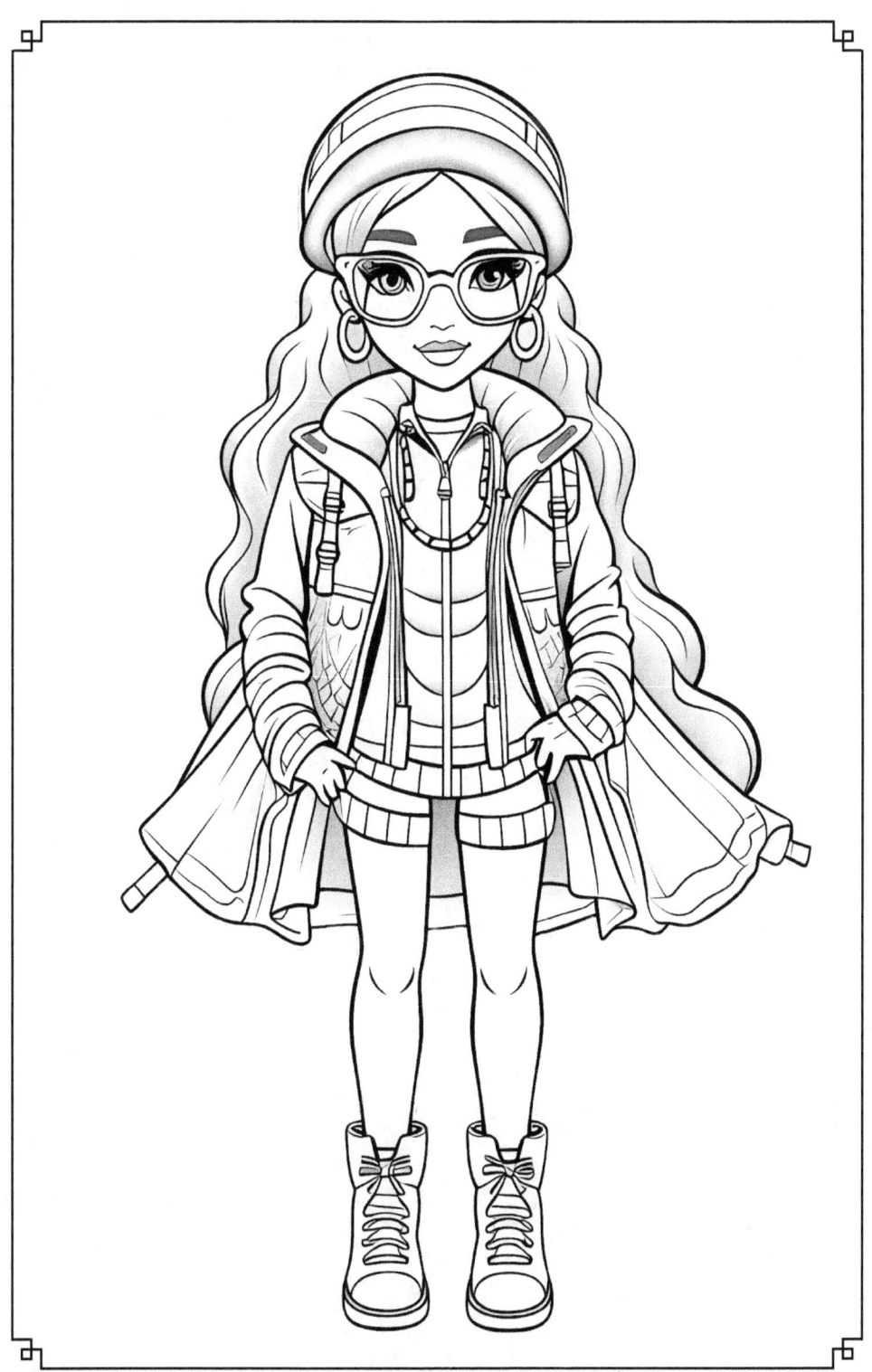

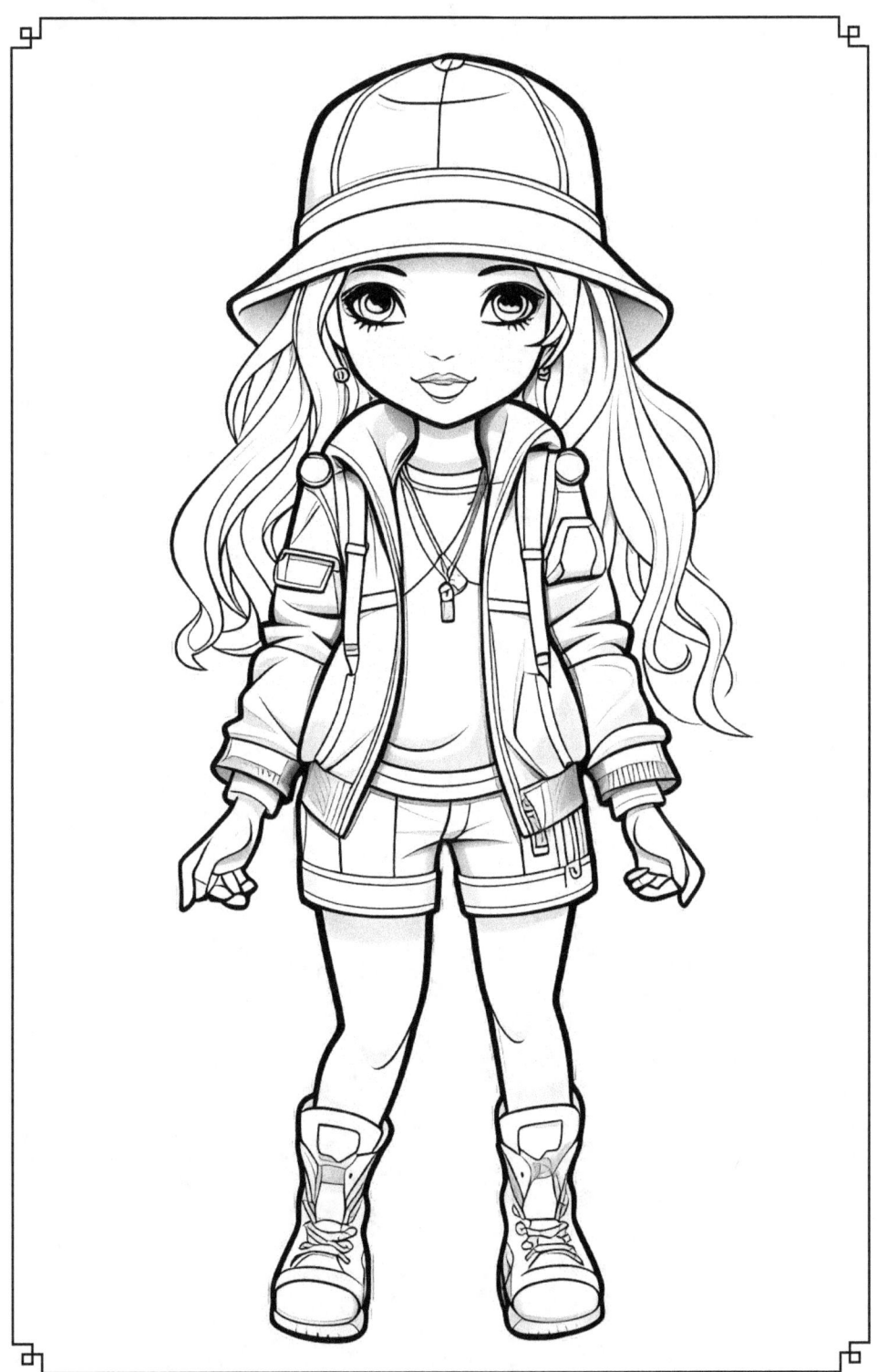

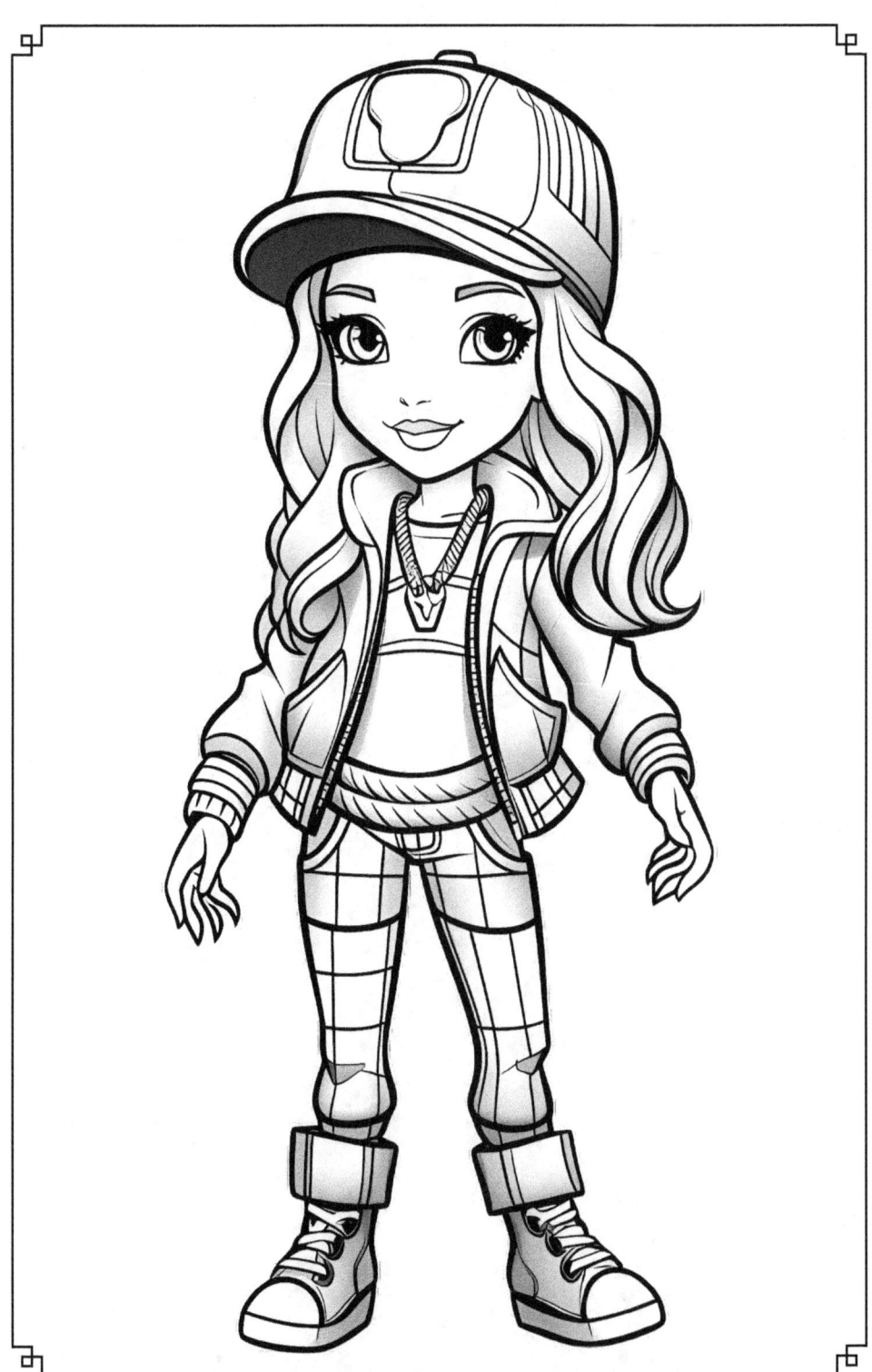

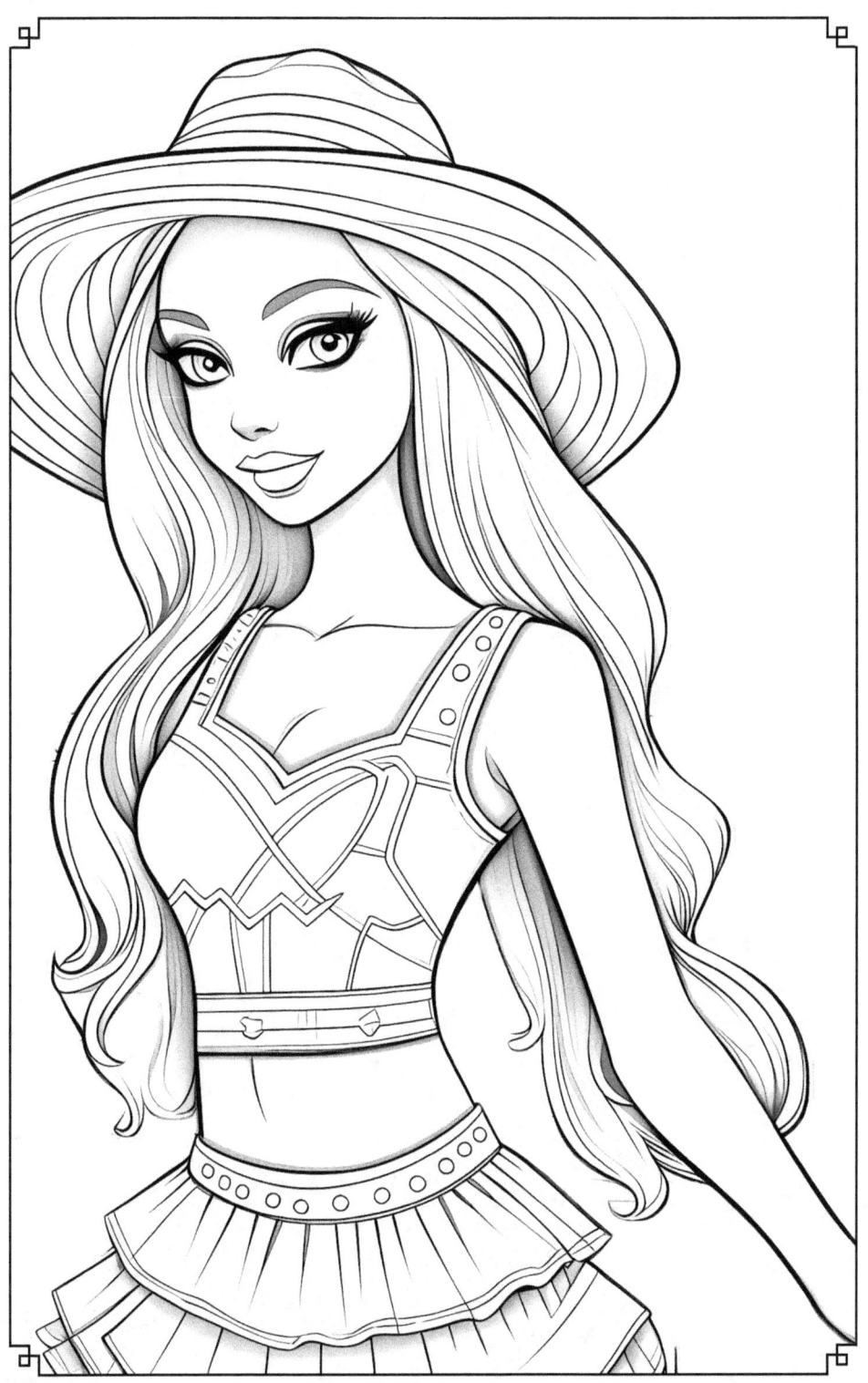

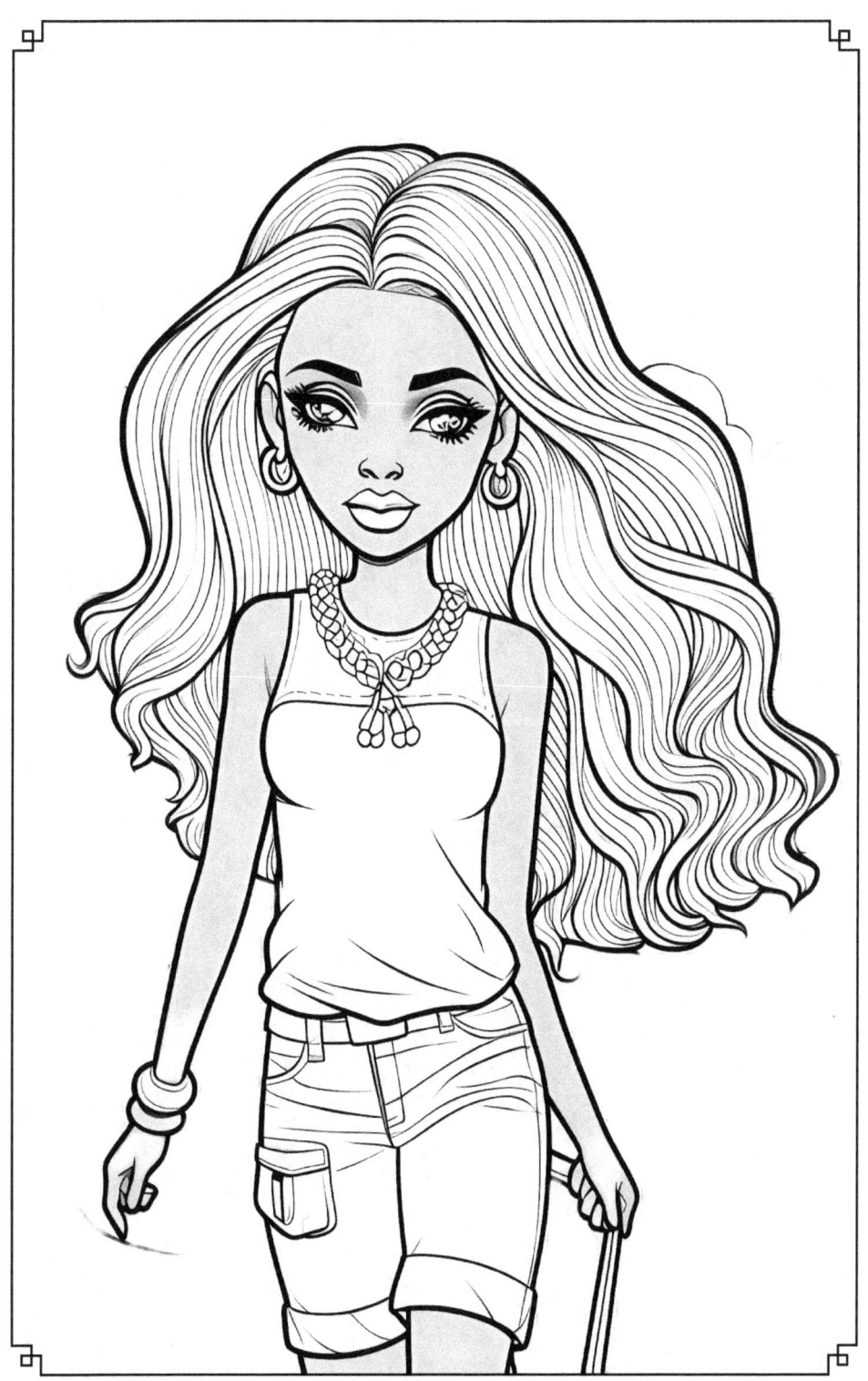

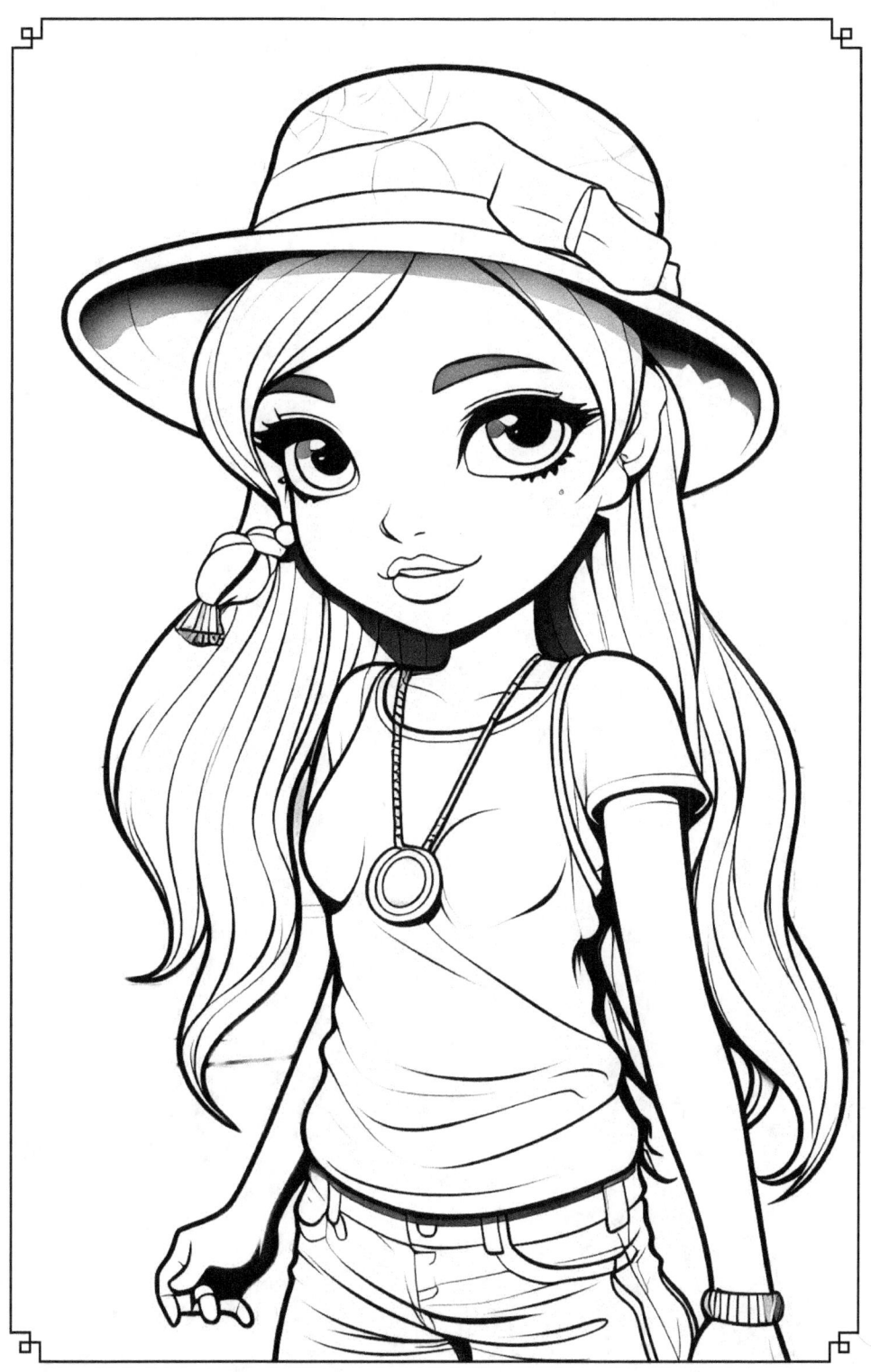

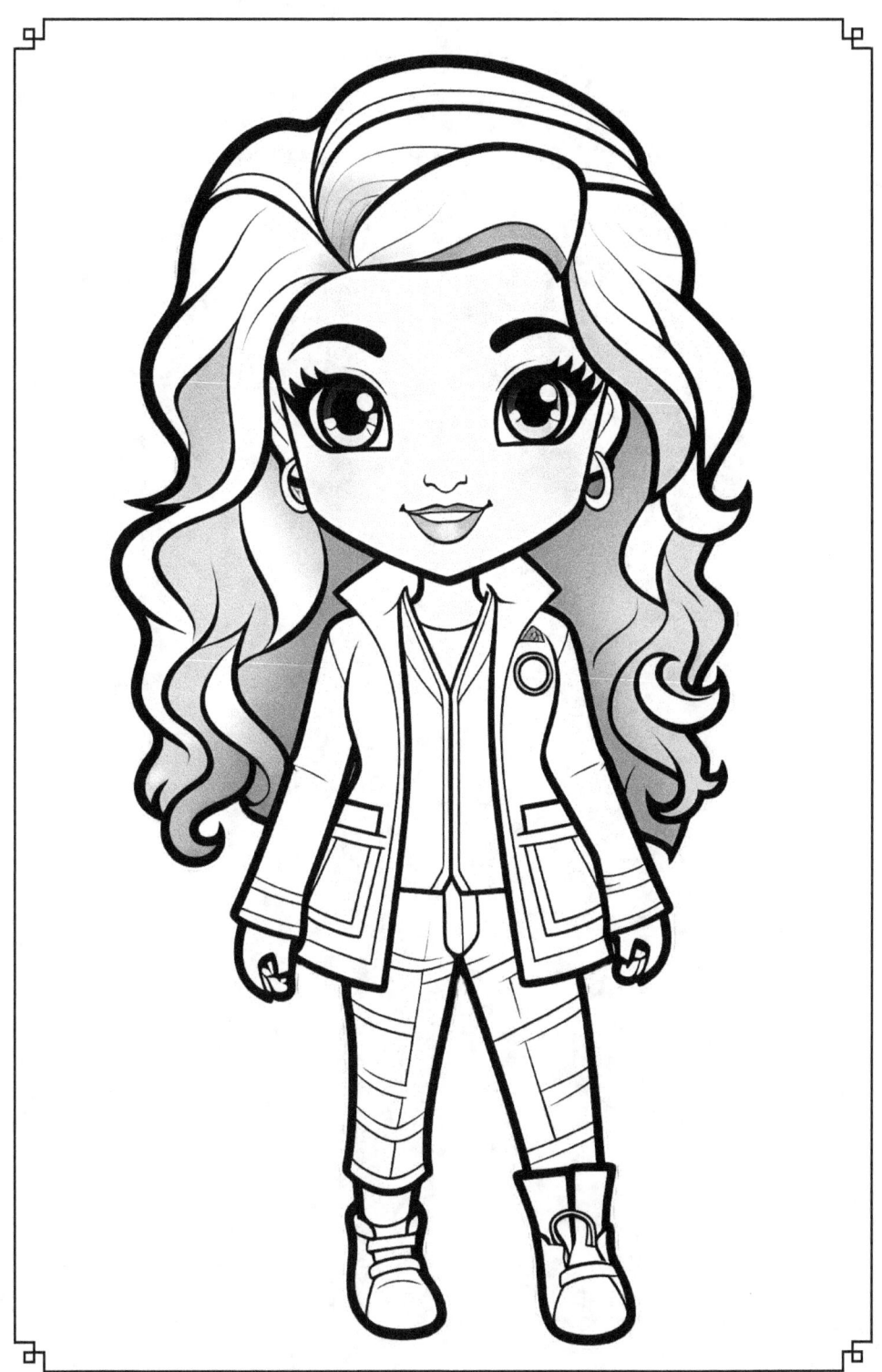

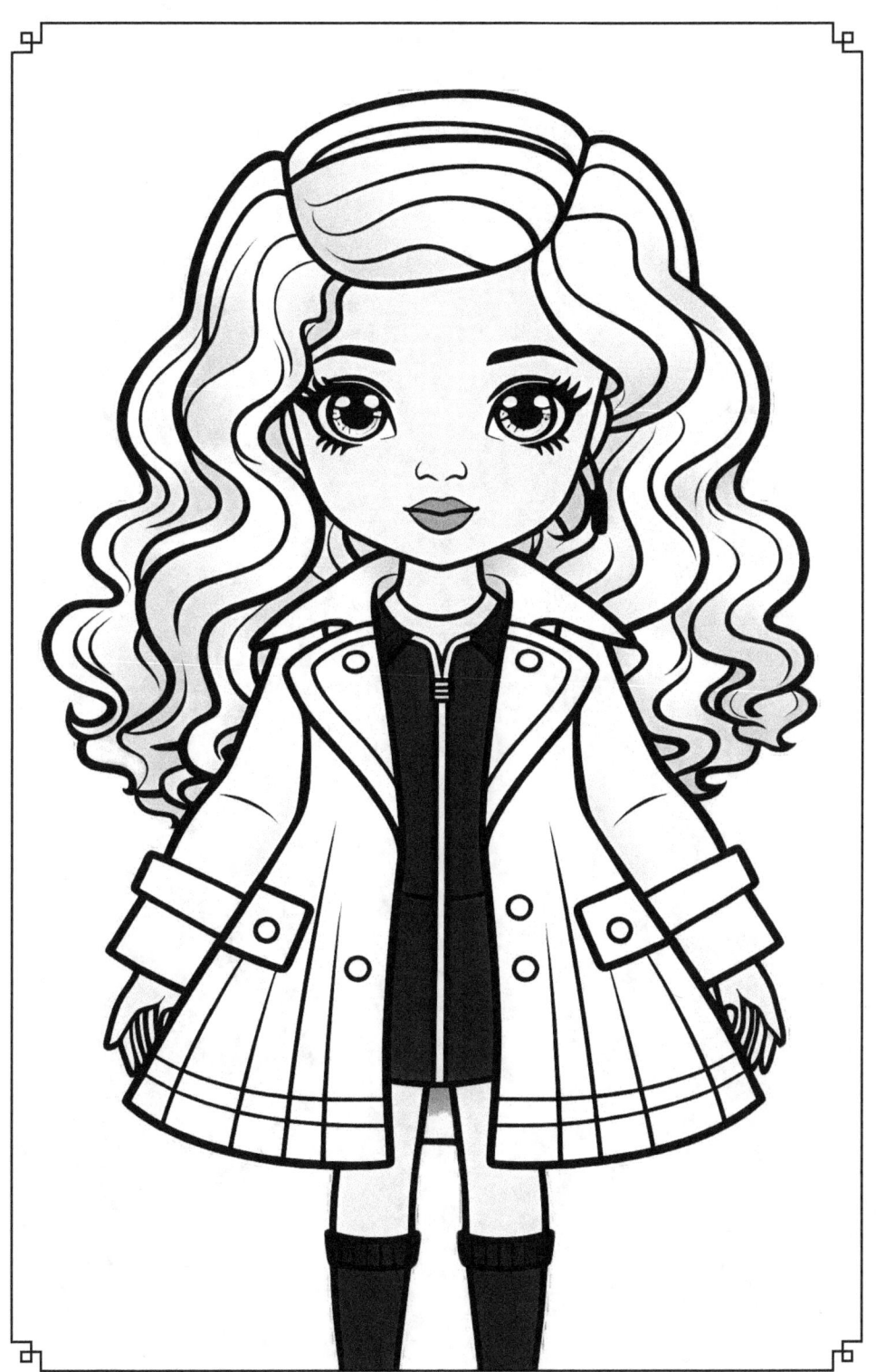

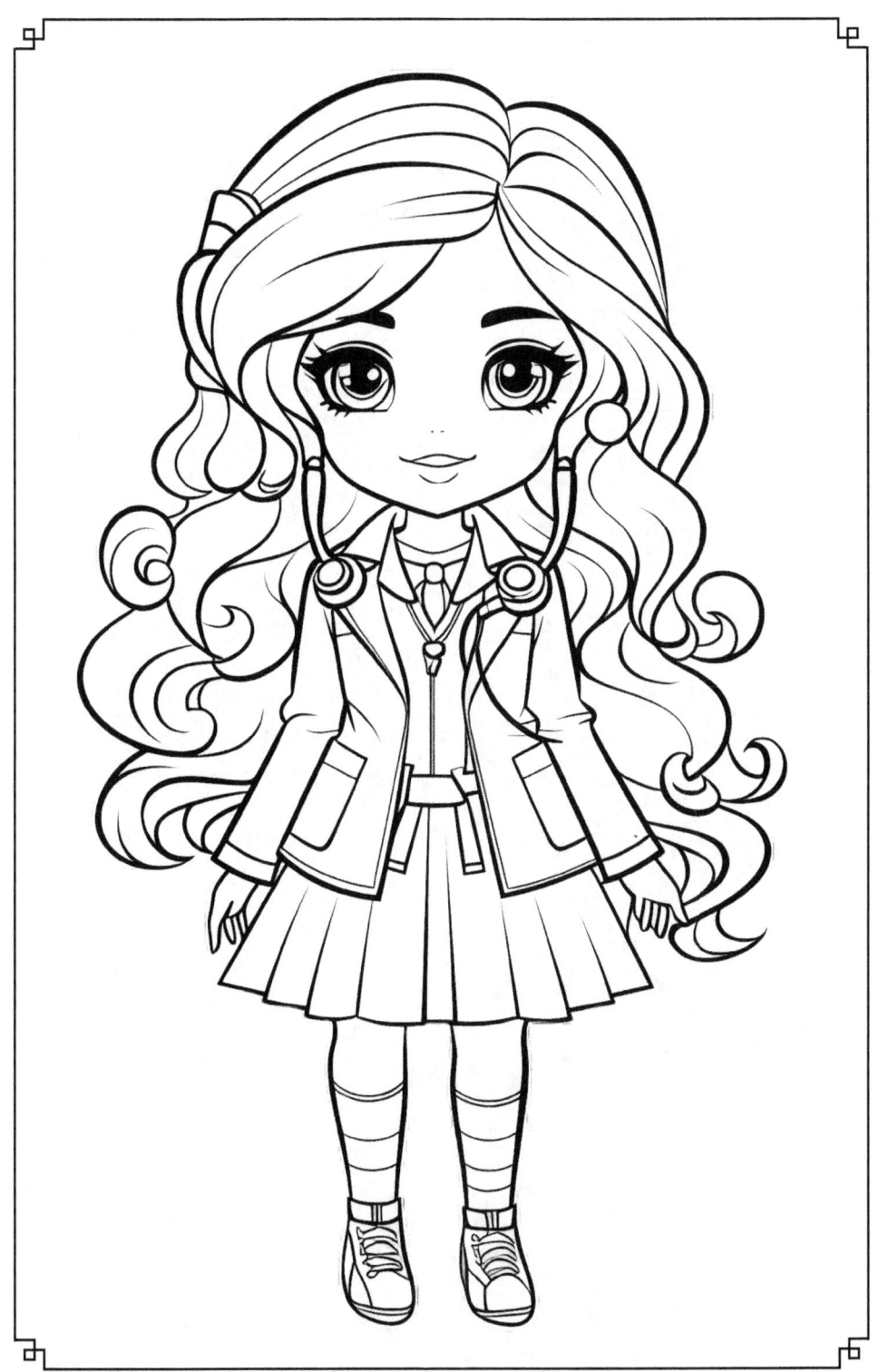

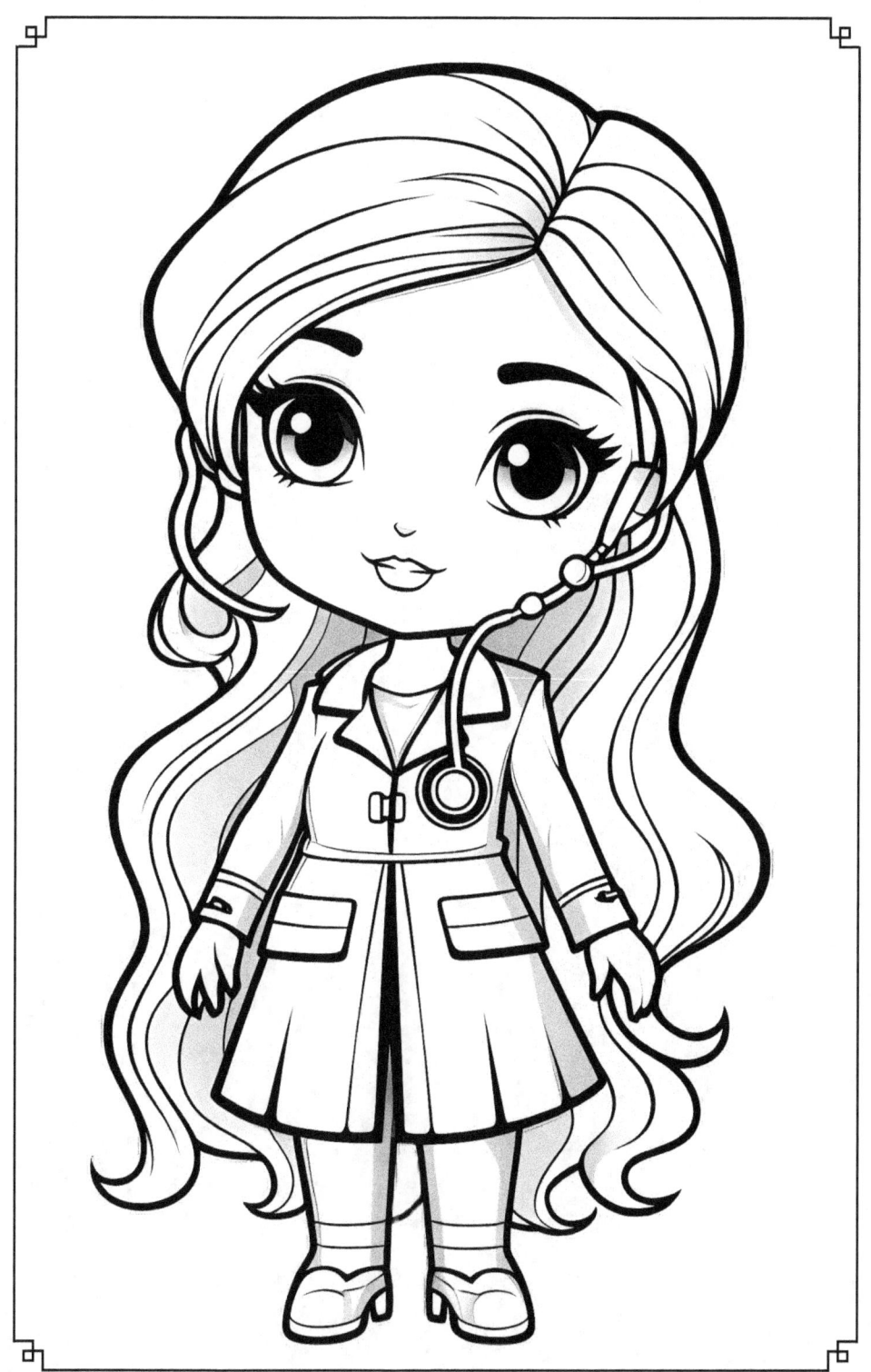

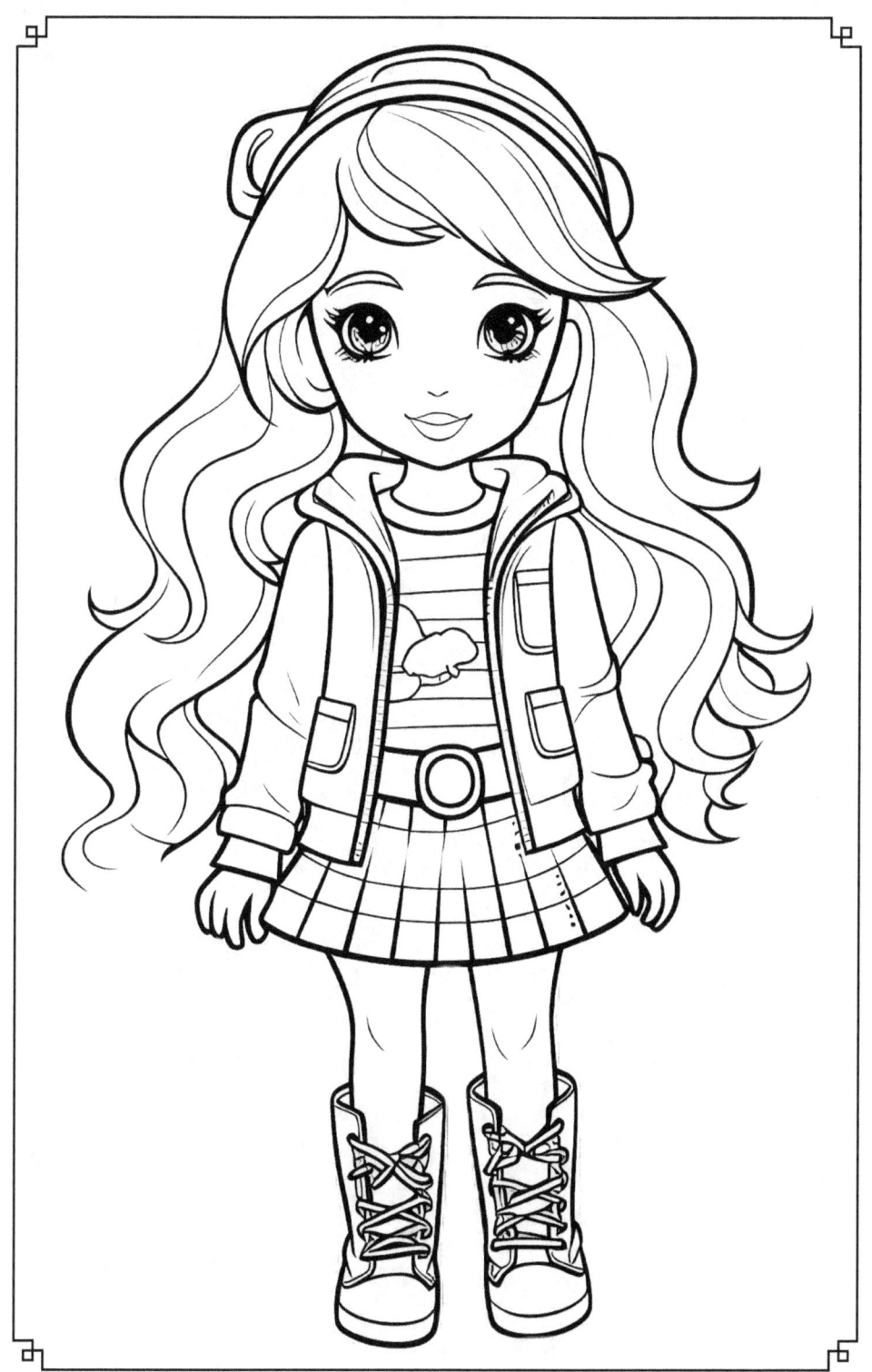

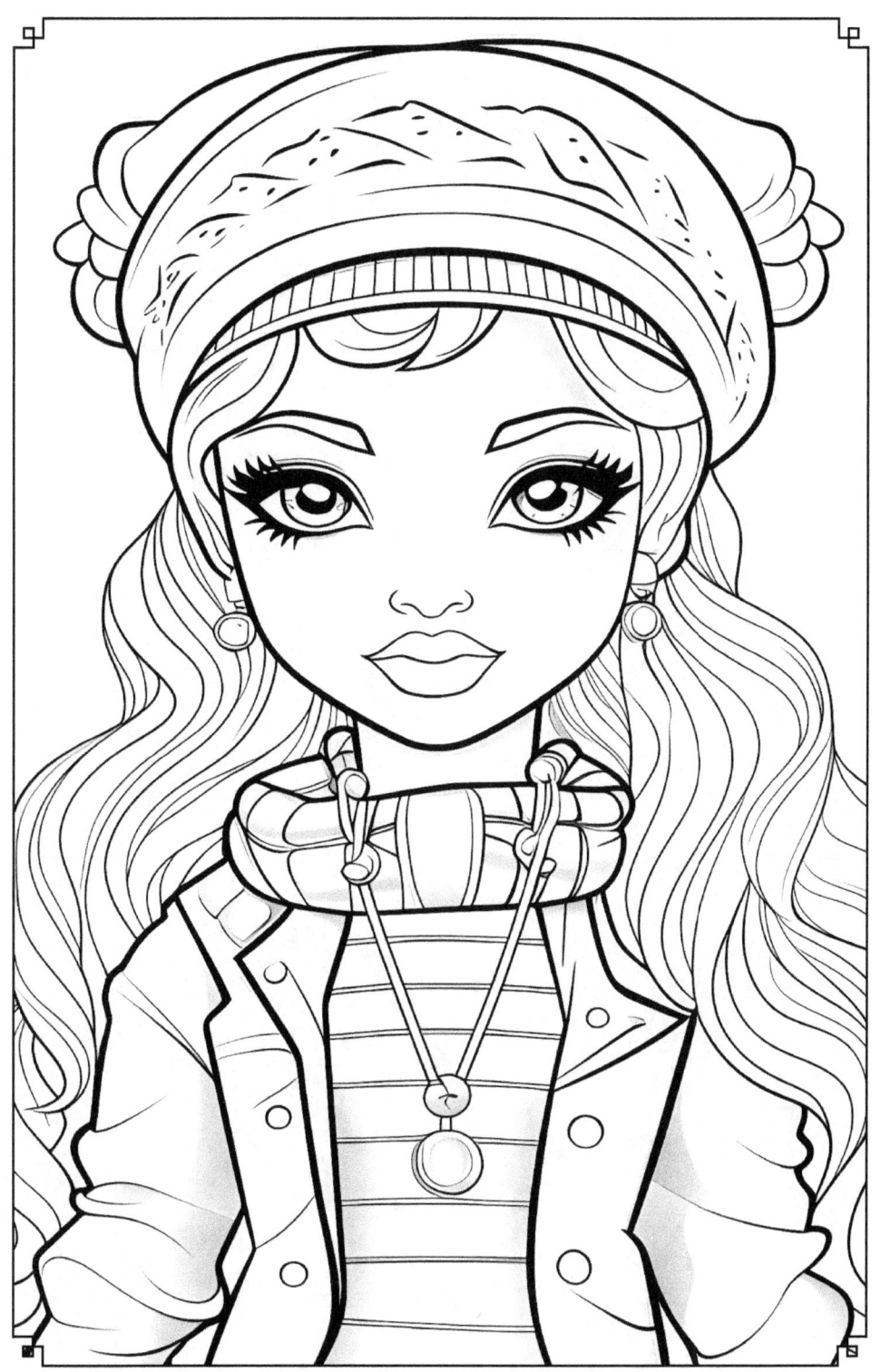

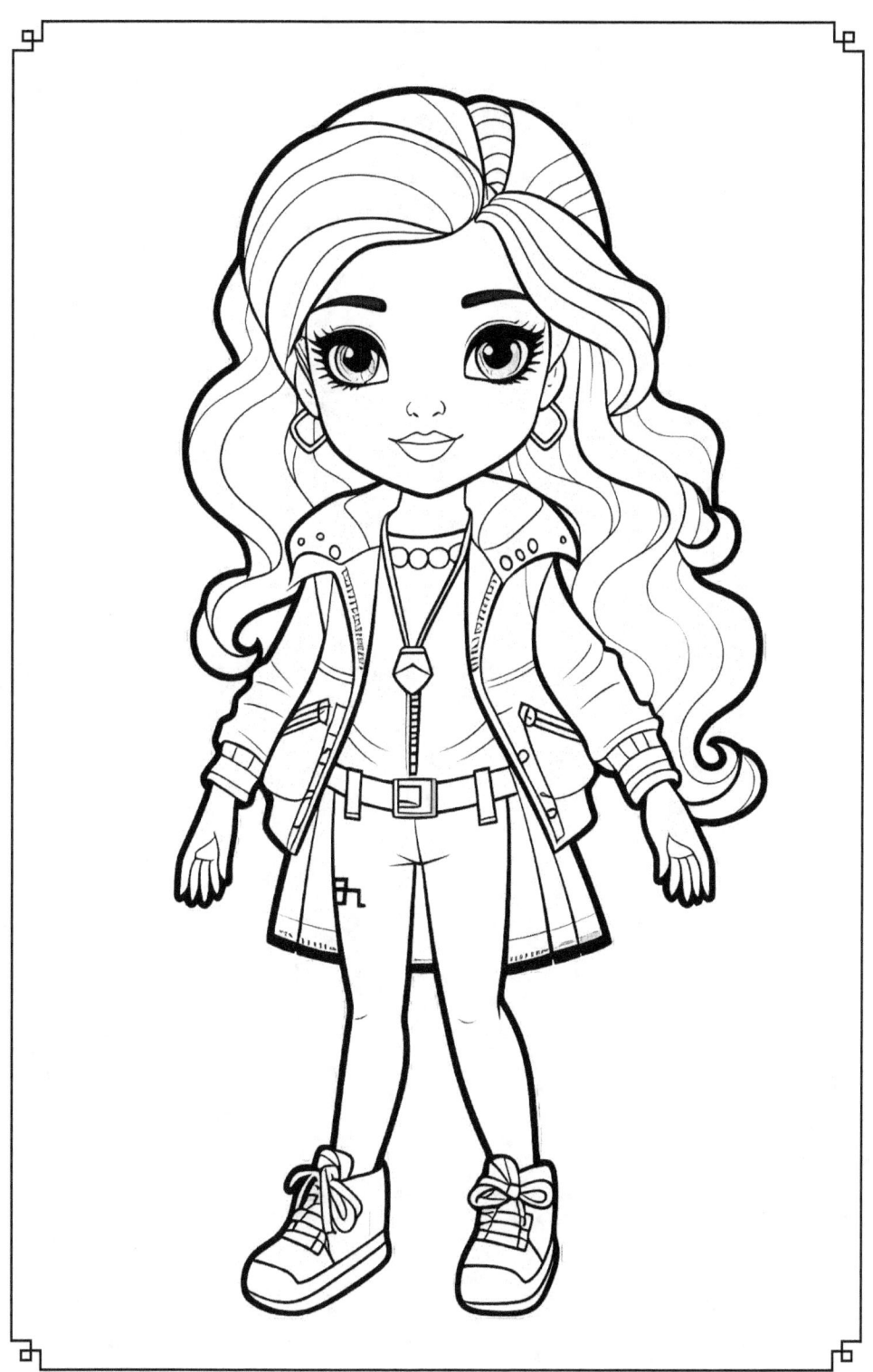

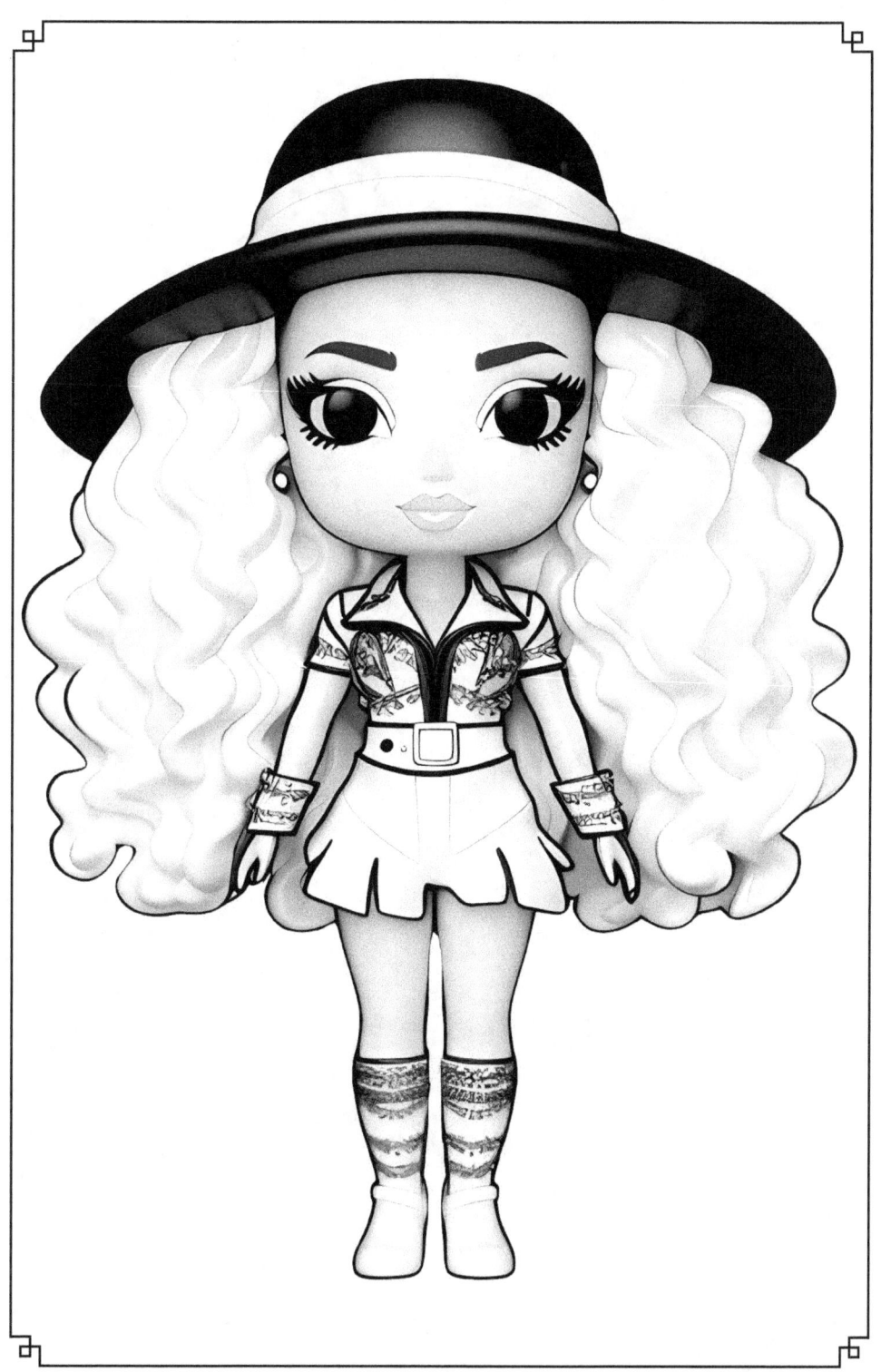

www.ingramcontent.com/pod-product-compliance
Lightning Source LLC
Chambersburg PA
CBHW062316290526
45794CB00005B/1821